MATCHING
FOOD & WINE
Classic and not so classic combinations

MICHEL ROUX JR

Photography by Tara Fisher

WEIDENFELD & NICOLSON

Contents

Introduction

LIKE ALL FRENCH children, I had my first sip of watered-down wine at about the age of ten, but I don't remember much about it other than it was red. On reflection, I doubt if my father would have watered down a Château Latour so it was probably a good old 'vin de table'.

This rite of passage is all part of growing up and learning the enjoyment that is to be had around a family table. I remember other times when the grand bottles came out and I was asked if I wanted a drop. When I shyly refused, my parents would shake their heads and ask what would become of their son if he didn't have a sip of this La Tâche, Domaine de la Romanée-Conti. 'Met ton nez la dedans' they would say as the glass was shoved into my face. 'Trempe les lèvres', which I have always thought of as a strange expression – I mean, what's the point in wetting your lips? I dread to think what my mother and father would have said if I had glugged down a full glass.

But this was all about initiation, respect and understanding of the good life as I see it, and as life in France still is today. I suppose my first memorable encounter with wine was sniffing its bouquet. I remember father swirling the wine around in the glass and with reverence placing it under my young, virginal nostrils. Château d'Yquem is memorable even at the tender age of 10 or 11. If only cough medicine could taste that good, I remember thinking!

I now find myself starting to teach my daughter about wine in the same way. In fact, I think it would be a crime not to. We recently went to visit a champagne house that makes quite exceptional wines. Gosset are small in comparison to the well-known names, but the style of their wine is big and flavoursome. You might think that any child would be bored stiff at the technicalities of making bubbly, but not Emily. She even pronounced her judgements at the tasting.

This attitude is common in France, and in Italy and Spain, where the pleasures of eating and drinking are taken seriously. Sitting around a table to eat still means something other than just re-fuelling, and nearly always includes a glass of wine.

Is it not extraordinary that something as humble as fermented grape juice could give so much pleasure? Admittedly not all wines are great, and some can be alarmingly awful. Thankfully wine is now no longer shrouded in mystery. Good wine is available and accessible to everybody.

This book is about food and drink, predominately wine. The pleasure to be had from consuming something delicious is unquantifiable, be it a plain ham sandwich with a glass of Beaujolais, or a roast snipe with a Côte Rôtie.

One does not have to fork out huge amounts of money to find good wine nowadays. There is a wide and varied choice, made easier to understand with the recent trend to label and call wines by their grape variety.

Many of the wines I have brought to your attention in this book are French. Like all good Frenchmen (OK, half French), I am proud and chauvinist. While I have come across some beautifully made wines from the USA, New Zealand, South Africa, Germany, Italy, Spain and Australia, I still feel that French wines are just that little bit special. However, I do admire wines from other countries and have listed many.

Continuing the family tradition, Emily Roux, 14, checks the nose of a fine 1997 Pauillac.

In the 1970s and 80s the French vignerons tended to rest on their laurels and produced a lot of bulk plonk with little character. But with the onslaught of wines from California and Australia, the French had to do something and thankfully they did. The New World wines were winning awards and plaudits from wine buffs everywhere and they were affordable, so the French producers went back to a small-is-better philosophy, with emphasis on quality rather than quantity. From the grand clarets all the way down to wines from the Languedoc region, the quality bar has been raised another notch.

In this book I look at what wine goes with what food. My suggestions may not always be the obvious choice, but most are accessible. I only mention a few specific domaines and châteaux and generally avoid mentioning specific vintages as I feel this only clouds the issue. If you want to take things further and check the best vintages, I suggest looking at any of the books by Michael Broadbent, Hugh Johnson or Jancis Robinson. Here, I'm simply looking at the combination of the different tastes of food and wine, and the style of the wine and predominant grape variety is more important than the individual bottle.

Ultimately this is all down to personal taste. If you want to drink a rich Australian Shiraz with a plate of seafood, so be it. But I can suggest something that will make both your food and your wine taste their best.

Decanting wine

WHY DECANT WINE? This is a question I'm often asked and there is no simple answer. The view of the so-called experts is that if a wine needs to breathe – that is to say, come into contact with oxygen to soften the tannins and release some of its hidden flavours – it needs decanting well before drinking. This might be 1–4 hours, depending on the wine.

The second reason for decanting comes from the true sense of the word decant – to pour a liquid from one container to another without disturbing sediment. This ensures that any sediment is left behind in the bottle so you can enjoy a clean wine without any bits in it!

Wines that need decanting

In general, wines that have sediment should be decanted. Open the bottle carefully and hold it over a candle or strong light as you gently pour the wine into a glass decanter. The light helps you see when the sediment is nearing the top of the bottle so you can stop pouring.

This is fine if the wine is less then 20 years old, but anything older than that may lose some of its delicate bouquet from this treatment. A rare old wine does not need to 'breathe' and should be opened only a short time before being consumed. Just gently pouring it into the glass should be enough. If by any chance the wine is a little closed or tight, a quick swirl in the glass should be enough to improve it.

Full-bodied young wines will probably benefit from a few hours in the decanter. This will soften any harsh tannins, release the hidden bouquet and allow the flavour to gain in complexity.

Some white wines also benefit from decanting for the same reasons. It is not unusual now to see sommeliers recommending just that, then vigorously swirling the wine in the decanter to release the finer complex flavours. If all of that sounds a little too pompous and complicated, I suggest you stick to drinking cask wine! Drinking wine is all about enjoyment and the pleasures it brings. Decanting is part and parcel of this. If you have a decanter, don't let it gather dust – use it.

Double decanting

Sometimes you may have a wine that needs decanting because of sediment, but you really want to show off its beautiful label or bottle. Double decanting is the solution. Pour the wine into a glass jug or any

In my view, if you have a beautiful decanter, use it. Certain whites as well as red wines can benefit from decanting.

clean container, leaving the sediment behind in the bottle. Discard the sediment and rinse the bottle carefully until it is totally clean. Pour the wine back into the bottle and it is ready to drink.

There are four types of wine that need decanting more often than others, mainly because of sediment or the need to breathe. These are:

- Vintage port, 12 years and older (this should always be decanted)

- Grand Bordeaux, 15 years and older

- New World Cabernets, 10 years and older

- Young Rhône whites and oaked New World Chardonnays

What makes a bad wine …and what makes a wine go bad?

There can be many reasons why a wine does not taste how it is meant to. One of the most common problems is 'corked' wine. This means that the cork used was faulty, badly dried or not properly treated before being used. The wine is then tainted and tends to smells of wet cardboard instead of fruit.

Oxidisation is another fault that can occur in wines. This is done deliberately to produce sherry and Madeira, but it is not something you expect in normal wines. Very often oxidised wine will have a brownish tinge and taste flat. This may come from a faulty cork, bad storage or a light wine being kept too long. If the wine is kept any longer it turns to vinegar – good for salads, but not for drinking.

Collecting, storing and serving wine

COLLECTING WINES FOR investment is one thing, drinking them is another – although with good judgement and a little knowledge a reasonable return can be expected over time. If you are not prepared to wait, then you can always drink your investment, which doesn't seem like such a bad option after all.

At Le Gavroche we invest literally thousands of pounds in wines that will not be ready to drink for another eight years or so. During that time the wine has to be cellared and looked after in the right conditions or it may become worthless. You can purchase wine for speculation without having to cellar it yourself. The wine can be kept 'in bond' for you or you can have it cellared in well-kept, professionally run cellars, at a price. One thing is for sure, collecting wine will never make you a millionaire, but it can be fun if you can resist the temptation to open the bottles!

As for keeping wines at home, most of us don't have proper cellars suitable for keeping wine in the right conditions. Table wine or wine that doesn't need to be aged can sit around a few months without too much harm coming to it, unless it's stored in direct sunlight and/or in a hot place. If you live in a flat, cupboards under stairs or against an outside wall are usually the best options, as long as there are no radiators nearby. What you are looking for is a somewhere with a constant, reasonably cool temperature. Fluctuations can kill a wine and warmer temperatures may prematurely age bottles, or in more extreme cases even 'cook' the wine. The ideal temperature should be 10–12 degrees Centigrade with a little humidity. If the air is too dry, the corks will suffer.

If you have space to store wine at home, make sure the temperature is reasonably stable and the air is not too dry.

To get the most out of your wine, whether young or vintage, it has to be served at the right temperature. If you serve a white wine too cold it will be dull and characterless. If it's not cold enough, its charm will have gone to the point of being lifeless. As for reds, if they are served too warm, the sensation of alcohol and tannins is increased and you lose out on fruit and bouquet. But if red wine is served too cold, it will be dull and insipid. This is all down to personal taste, however. These guidelines do not legislate for those who like to put ice cubes in a glass of the finest Chardonnay or want their Claret so warm it's almost steaming – and believe me, I have seen it all.

One thing I have learned from being half English and half French is that the French like their wines colder than the English do. I am forever cupping my hands around the glass in even the best restaurants in France to bring the temperature up by a couple of degrees. Red wine should be brought to room temperature, 18 degrees Centigrade, by being in the room for a couple of hours beforehand.

If you need to chill a white wine in a hurry, put it in an ice bucket, or any container that's big and tall enough, with ice, a handful of coarse salt and just enough water to surround the bottle. In ten minutes your wine will be ready to drink.

Temperature	Wine
4–9°C	Sweetest white dessert wines (the sweeter the wine, the colder it should be), sparkling wines
8–12°C	Champagnes (vintages nearer 12°C), dry white wines, sherry, muscats, rosés
10–14°C	Table wine, Beaujolais, lighter reds, German and Alsace Pinot Noir, Tempranillo
13–15°C	Port, Madeira, fine whites such as Montrachet or Corton-Charlemagne
14–16°C	Côtes du Rhônes, Zinfandel, Chianti
15–17°C	Red Burgundy
16–19°C	Claret and best Merlot wines

Glassware

THE ENJOYMENT OF wines can only be enhanced by using the right glasses. After all, if you go to the trouble to lay the table beautifully and cook a delicious dinner, it would be shame not to serve the wine in the correct vessel. Pottery and silver are definitely out of the question, coloured glass hides the natural beauty of the wine and thick goblets should be kept for picnics.

The ideal glass should be thin and have a stem so that you can swirl the wine without spilling or warming it. A 300ml/10oz glass is a good average size and some shapes are better suited to some wines. For example, a smaller glass with a slightly closed lip at the top helps to concentrate the bouquet of white wines, while larger, balloon-shaped glasses are more appropriate for silky red wines.

Remember that a glass should never be filled more than half full to get the most out of the wine and you do not need to spend a fortune on

This page from left to right:
Champagne
Chardonnay
Sauvignon Blanc
Gewürztraminer
Montrachet

a collection of glasses to enjoy different grape varieties. However, if you do decide to invest, I think Riedel glassware is the best. This company has designed glasses for almost every type of wine imaginable. Each glass has been tried and tested to get the best from the wine. For most of us, though, glasses for white, red, Champagne and dessert wines are more than enough. The champagne glasses should be flutes or tulips to allow the bubbles to rise from a single point and concentrate the delicate bouquet. The old-fashioned saucers make the fizz dissipate too quickly and should only be used for fruit salads! The dessert or fortified wine glass should be the same shape as a white wine glass but half the size.

Wash glasses in hot soapy water and rinse thoroughly, as even the slightest trace of detergent will play havoc with wine. Keep glasses upright and cover with a clean cloth or tea towel. If glasses are left upside down, the air trapped inside will go stale and taint the glass.

This page from left to right:
Burgundy
Syrah/Shiraz
Chianti Classico
Bordeaux
Cognac

Matching Food and Wine

NEVER BELIEVE ANYONE who tells you that certain foods don't go with wine until you've tried them for yourself. A good match of food and wine is a joy, and a pleasure that everyone can appreciate. There's no need to break the bank to find a good wine – although when you do it should be a memorable event. The work has been done for you, from the nurturing of the vines to the ageing, blending and bottling. All you have to do is serve the wine at the right temperature and with the right dish. So how do you choose what to serve? Ask yourself what kind of wines you like, then consider the texture and style of the food and how it is prepared and sauced. Think of wine as a seasoning. It livens up not only the palate but also the senses. And remember that life really is too short to drink bad wine.

CLASSIC COMBINATIONS

These are all tried and tested partners – foods and wines that always go well with each other.

FOODS	WINES
Spanish tapas	Manzanilla sherry
Pasta with white truffles	Barolo
Oysters	Champagne Blanc de Blancs or Guinness
Sweet Charentais melon	Port or Pineau des Charentes
Roast leg of lamb	Bordeaux – Pomerol or Pauillac
Spicy curry	Cold India pale ale
Well-hung game	Côte Rôtie
Farmhouse Stilton	Port, tawny or vintage
Goat cheese such as Crottin de Chavignol	Loire Valley, Sauvignon, Pouilly Fumé
Poached apricots	Tokaji Aszu (sweet Hungarian), 5 Puttonyos
Dark bitter chocolate	Maury 1928 Solera
Tarte tatin	Sweet bottled cider
Sole meunière	Chablis

DIFFICULT FOODS

There are certain food items that react badly to wine and must be given careful consideration.

Artichokes Make any wine taste metallic, although less so if cooked or in rich meat sauce
Asparagus Leaves a bitter taste in the month, although a cream truffle vinaigrette helps to nullify this
Egg yolks and hollandaise-based sauces Egg yolk coats the taste buds and leaves you unable to taste
Hot spices A mouth that's on fire will obviously not be in condition to appreciate good wines
Ice creams and sorbets Both egg-based and freezing, they anaesthetise the taste buds
Smoked food Dry foods such as hams are not so bad, but oily fish can be a major problem as it coats the mouth with a film that leaves you unable to taste anything else
Vinaigrette Anything with wine vinegar in a high quantity will not complement the wine, but a little lemon juice is passable. A drop of acidity in foods brings out the taste, so a little give and take is needed here.

NOT SO CLASSIC COMBINATIONS

Here are some less familiar combinations that may surprise you but are just as good.

FOODS	WINES
Salami and smoked ham	German Spätlese wine
Sardines on toast	Dry white English wine
Singapore Laksa	Young Condrieu
Cold seafood soup with salt cod	Tavel rosé or Bellet rosé, 5 or 6 years old
Roast grouse	Montepulciano (Italian red), 10 years old
Roast turkey and trimmings	Adelaide Hills Pinot Noir
Wild strawberries with aged Balsamic vinegar	Moscato d'Asti
Figs and Parma ham	Young South African Pinotage
Camembert and Brie	Crémant d'Alsace
Roquefort	Chateau d'Yquem
Munster cheese with cumin seeds	Newcastle Brown Ale
Lime cheesecake	Old Riesling
Pure dark chocolate	Old sweet Madeira Malmsey

Pre dinner

What happens before a meal sets the tone for what you are about to receive. Gathering round with new friends or simply getting together with family, drink in hand, brings you into a nice relaxed mood, ready for the joys of eating and drinking. An hour is ideal for pre-dinner drinks, allowing ample time for the chef or host to make the last-minute preparations for the meal. Serve light snacks or canapés as there is nothing worse than drinking alcohol on an empty stomach. Not only does it go straight to your head, but it also blunts the appetite. Avoid peanuts and the like, though, as they will kill the taste of any decent wine you are serving. If you only have time to serve a packet snack, gourmet, hand-cooked crisps or pretzels are a safe bet. But don't overdo it – two types are more than enough. Don't serve them all at once and make them last. Think quality not quantity.

To open the appetite as the French say, you need something that will stimulate the taste buds. Champagne is ideal and a good sparkling wine also works well, but stick to dry or brut. In general, dry, bitter drinks make you hungry. Unless you're serving just one type of drink, such as a wine, most snacks will go with most drinks. Non-vintage Champagne, for example, is an ideal partner for little fishy or cheesy snacks and will not be overpowered by a spicy spring roll.

Krug Collection 1964
This Champagne embodies the Krug character. Smooth, flowery and slightly Madeirised,
it is full of life despite its age and proves that a good Champagne can age beautifully.
Pre dinner, serve with something very delicate, such as cheese straws.

Cheese Straws, Poppy Straws, Almond Straws

Light, crisp and buttery, puff pastry is a perfect match for most aperitifs. You can flavour these puff pastry straws with almost anything you like once you've got the knack — try herbes de Provence and paprika as well as the suggestions below.

SERVES 4

300g puff pastry (choose
   best-quality fresh puff
   pastry made with butter)
3 egg yolks
140g grated cheese, such as
   Parmesan, mature
   Cheddar or Gruyère
1 tsp paprika and/or chilli
   powder or to taste
4 tbsp poppy seeds
freshly grated nutmeg
120g nibbed almonds
1 tbsp cumin

Preheat the oven to 200°C/gas 6. Lightly dust the work surface with flour and roll out the puff pastry to a thickness of 2–3mm, keeping it as square as possible. Trim the edges. Beat the egg yolks and wash over the pastry with a brush.

For cheese straws, liberally sprinkle the pastry with cheese, then dust with paprika and/or a little chilli. For poppy straws, sprinkle with poppy seeds and a touch of nutmeg. And for almond straws, use nibbed almonds and cumin. Gently press your chosen topping so that it adheres to the pastry.

Cut the pastry into strips 20cm long by 1.5cm wide. Pick up each strip and twirl five or six times to make spirals. Lay the strips on a non-stick baking mat or a lightly greased baking tray, keeping them straight and pressing hard at each end to fix and hold them down. Bake in the preheated oven for 10–12 minutes until golden.

WINES

Champagne would be my choice, but lager, with its slightly bitter taste, certainly stimulates the appetite and goes well with cheese. If you want to drink spirits, a good whisky with little neutral mineral water, no ice, also works a treat.

CHAMPAGNE BRUT
PILSNER LAGER
SINGLE MALT WHISKY

Salt Cod and Crab Fritters

Soak the cod overnight. Next day, leave under a stream of cold water for another couple of hours to remove the saltiness and reconstitute. Drain, dry and remove all bones. Cut the cod into small dice and add to the crab, garlic and onion. Make a batter with the egg, flour, chilli and milk, making sure there are no lumps, then add to the crab and cod. Leave to rest for an hour. Using a tablespoon dipped in water, shape into little patties. Heat the oil in a deep fryer or big saucepan. Drop the fritters into the hot oil for 3–4 minutes, turning them over to give an even colour. Drain on kitchen towel and serve warm.

For the dipping sauce, mix the sugar, water and vinegar in a pan and bring to the boil. Add the clove and chilli. Leave to cool.

WINES
Salt cod and chilli have strong flavours and need strong bubbles and a good acidity. A good refreshing alternative would be a Chablis with its distinctive powerful aroma.

NON-VINTAGE CHAMPAGNE

CAVA

CHABLIS

MAKES 20–25 FRITTERS

250g salt cod

175g cleaned white crab meat, preferably claw meat

1 garlic clove, peeled and finely chopped

1 onion, peeled and finely chopped

1 egg

100g plain flour

1 tsp chilli powder

65ml milk

vegetable oil for deep frying, enough for oil about 15cm deep in the pan

Dipping sauce

1 tbsp caster sugar

4 tbsp water

1 tbsp white wine vinegar

1 clove

1 red chilli, sliced

Mini Fish Balls

These little fish cakes are potato based but still very fishy. You can also make larger versions for a starter or main course. My favourite for this recipe is cod, but it works well with salmon, too.

SERVES 6

360g cod or hake, skinned
  and boned
butter for greasing
salt and pepper
2 shallots, peeled and finely
  chopped
100ml dry white wine
200g potatoes, boiled and
  mashed
1 bunch of flat-leaf parsley
1 tbsp crème fraîche
flour for dredging
2 eggs
100g dry breadcrumbs
vegetable oil for frying

Place the fish in a buttered ovenproof dish, season well and scatter over the chopped shallots. Pour in the wine, cover and bake in a hot oven, 220°C/gas 7, for 8–10 minutes. The fish should be just cooked and still a little pink inside. Leave to cool. Collect all the fishy juices and reduce these over high heat until syrupy.

Flake the fish into the mashed potato with the shallots. Fold in the chopped parsley, crème fraîche and the reduced cooking juices. Don't make the mixture too moist – it needs to be firm enough so you can shape little balls. Keep them small – this quantity should make about 30. Roll each fish ball in flour, then egg and finally the breadcrumbs. Fry in vegetable oil in a large pan for a few minutes until golden. Drain on kitchen towel and serve immediately.

WINES

As you will have gathered already, Champagne is my favourite aperitif, but a dry Vouvray or an Entre Deux Mers both have the depth and acidity needed for this fish dish.

NON-VINTAGE CHAMPAGNE BRUT
DRY VOUVRAY
ENTRE DEUX MERS

Celeriac Remoulade and Smoked Duck

The celeriac remoulade is even better after a couple of days in the fridge. Choose a smoked duck supreme that has not been too dried. Don't serve it too cold or the flavour will be lost.

Start by making the mayonnaise. Whisk together the egg yolks, Dijon mustard, lemon juice, salt and pepper. Gradually whisk in the vegetable oil, a little at a time, until all the oil is incorporated and the mixture is completely emulsified.

Peel the celeriac, taking care to remove enough of the skin as it can be woody. Using a vegetable slicer, cut the celeriac into very fine julienne strips. Add these to the mayonnaise and stir in the wholegrain mustard. Leave to sit for at least a couple of hours so the celeriac has time to soften.

Slice the baguettes into about 30 bite-size slices and toast both sides. Remove some of the fat from the duck supreme and slice very thinly to make least 30 pieces. Twirl a little remoulade on to each toast with a fork, add a strip of smoked duck and decorate with some sliced spring onion.

WINES

Most smoked and salty food goes well with sherry. Communard – a version of kir made from chilled Beaujolais and Cassis – is another delicious way to start festivities. It's a drink for any time of day that the Lyonnais tend to quaff with abandon! Failing that, a chilled Pineau fortified wine would also go well with smoked duck.

FINO SHERRY
COMMUNARD (BEAUJOLAIS AND CRÈME DE CASSIS)
PINEAU DES CHARENTES RED

SERVES 6
2 egg yolks
½ tbsp Dijon mustard
juice of 1 lemon
salt and pepper
200ml vegetable oil
1 celeriac, about 500g
½ tbsp wholegrain mustard
2 mini baguettes
1 smoked duck supreme
2 spring onions, sliced
  very thinly

Crispy Chorizo Rolls

The only problem with these rolls is that once you start eating them, you can't stop. Crisp, spicy and salty, they are delicious and guaranteed to get the juices going. If you can't get brique pastry, use spring roll pastry.

SERVES 8
6 spicy cooking chorizo,
   about 80g each
10 sheets of brique pastry
   (North African paper-
   thin pancakes)
1 tbsp plain flour
vegetable oil

Cut the chorizo in half lengthways, then cut each half in three strips. Roll each chorizo strip in just enough brique pastry to go round twice. Close the edges and ends with a little paste made with flour and water, pressing well to make sure they are properly sealed.

Heat the vegetable oil in a deep fryer or large pan. Before adding the chorizo rolls, test the temperature of the oil by dropping in a small piece of bread. If it sizzles and turns golden the oil is ready. Deep fry the rolls for a few minutes until golden. Alternatively, brush them with olive oil and bake in a hot oven, 200°C/gas 6, for 5–6 minutes until crispy.

WINES

Sherry and tapas-style food is a classic combination. Amontillado, with its warm, tawny colour and deep flavour from years of ageing in wooden casks, is deceptively high in alcohol so beware. A dry chilled white port or vermouth would also be good partners for this dish.

AMONTILLADO SHERRY
DRY WHITE PORT
DRY WHITE VERMOUTH

Blinis with Caviar

These little black diamonds of the sea are an extravagant luxury, but worth every penny. You could, however, use a good quality salmon roe or alternate black and red caviar.

MAKES 20 BLINIS
15g fresh yeast or one
   sachet of dried yeast
200ml lukewarm milk
50g wholewheat flour
3 eggs
75g strong bread flour
75g rye flour
pinch of salt
vegetable oil

Garnish
125ml whipping cream
125ml crème fraîche
200g (or more!) caviar
4 spring onions, sliced into
   thin slivers

First make the blinis. Dissolve the yeast in the milk. Mix in the wholewheat flour, cover and leave to ferment in a draught-free place for an hour. Mix 1 whole egg and 2 yolks with the strong bread flour, rye flour and salt, and cover. Leave for an hour, then add to the yeast mixture. Whisk the remaining 2 egg whites until stiff and fold into the mixture. Heat a non-stick pan greased with a little vegetable oil. To make small blinis, drop in a spoonful of the mixture, cook for a minute or two, then flip over to cook the other side. Continue until all the mixture is used up.

Garnish Whisk the cream until it forms peaks and fold in the crème fraîche. Pipe or spoon some of this mixture on to each blini. Then spoon on a generous amount of caviar and decorate with a sliver of spring onion.

WINES
Flavoured vodkas, such as chilli or lemon, work well, but can blunt your appetite if you drink too much. Bollinger, with its depth of flavour and strength of character, is the best style of Champagne to serve with caviar.

ICED VODKA
FULL-BODIED CHAMPAGNE (SUCH AS BOLLINGER)

Duck Scratchings

These are definitely not for anyone on a diet. Sold in charcuteries in Lyons, they are also made with pork, but duck is my favourite.

Cut the duck skin into strips 3cm long. Place them in a wide pan with enough water to cover by about 1cm. Add the rosemary and fat. Bring to a gentle simmer and cook until all the water has evaporated. There now should be enough fat in the pan to cover the scratchings. If not, add a little more fat and continue to simmer gently, but be careful as the duck scratchings may spit and pop. When the strips have turned a light golden brown and are perfectly crisp, drain and sprinkle with salt and pepper.

WINES

Communard is a mix of chilled Beaujolais and Cassis, a favourite in the 'bouchons' (small traditional restaurants) in Lyons. The Bugey region northeast of Lyon produces a lightly sparkling rosé made from the Gamay grape – different and refreshing.

COMMUNARD (BEAUJOLAIS AND CRÈME DE CASSIS)
CERDON DU BUGEY

SERVES 6

1kg duck skin from the breast, preferably from an Aylesbury or a Canard Gras (duck raised for foie gras)
1 sprig rosemary
2 tbsp duck or goose fat
coarse sea salt
freshly ground black pepper

Chilli Coconut Fried Tiger Prawns

You can taste the tropics in this recipe. Just close your eyes and dream…

SERVES 8

24 raw tiger prawns
250g grated (desiccated)
  coconut
2 or 3 dried red chillies or
  more to taste, chopped
salt and pepper
200g cornflour
3 egg whites
vegetable oil for frying

Remove the heads and shells of the prawns, leaving the tails on. De-vein to remove the intestines. Mix together the coconut and chopped chillies and season with salt and pepper.

Heat some oil in a deep fryer or large pan. Dip each prawn into the cornflour and then into the beaten egg whites. Finally coat in the seasoned coconut and chopped chillies. Deep fry the prawns until golden brown. Drain on kitchen towel and serve piping hot.

WINES

For me, a dry, cold sherry is an ideal partner for seafood and chilli. Strong flavours need to be balanced by equally bold wines. German Riesling is fragrant, with enough acidity to cope with these flavours and a classic Kir Royale is equally at home with mild chilli.

FINO SHERRY
GERMAN RIESLING
KIR ROYALE (CHAMPAGNE AND CRÈME DE CASSIS)

Cheese-filled Choux Buns

Also called gougère, these little buns are originally from Burgundy. You can experiment with different cheeses, but stick to hard, mature varieties, such as Mimolette, Beaufort or even Caerphilly.

Preheat the oven to 220°C/gas 7. Bring the milk and water to the boil with the butter, salt and sugar. Take off the heat and immediately beat in the flour with a spatula until smooth. Put the pan back on the heat and cook for a minute or two, beating well with the spatula.

Take the pan off the heat and beat in the eggs one at a time, again using a spatula, until smooth. Take a non-stick baking sheet and using a teaspoon or a piping bag, divide the mixture into small round balls, about 2.5cm wide. Sprinkle with the grated cheese. Bake in the preheated oven for 10 minutes, then open the door briefly to let out the steam. Close the oven door and continue to cook for another 10 minutes until crisp. Take out and cool on a wire rack.

The filling is a thick béchamel sauce. Melt the butter in a pan and add the flour. Cook gently for 5 minutes, stirring continuously and making sure that the mixture does not colour. Gently pour on the milk and whisk well to avoid lumps. Continue to boil until the sauce is well cooked. Take off the heat, season to taste with salt, pepper and spices, and add the grated cheese. Make a little hole at the base of each choux bun. Using a piping bag and nozzle, fill with the béchamel. These are best served warm and can be reheated in a moderate oven.

WINES

With their clean tastes, Champagne and Cremant de Bourgogne both work beautifully with creamy cheese. In fact, in tasting panels, Champagne has come out as a surprisingly good all-rounder for serving with cheese.

CREMANT DE BOURGOGNE
CHAMPAGNE (YOUNG OR OLD)

MAKES 25–30 BUNS
100ml milk
150ml water
100g butter cut into small cubes
1 pinch of salt
2 pinch of caster sugar
150g plain sifted flour
4 eggs
100g grated mature Cheddar

Filling
60g butter
1½ tbsp plain flour
300ml milk
salt, pepper, cayenne and nutmeg
100g grated hard cheese such as Mimolette, Beaufort and Caerphilly

Joseph Drouhin

Montrachet

GRAND CRU
APPELLATION CONTROLÉE

Marquis de Laguiche

MIS EN BOUTEILLE PAR JOSEPH DROUHIN
NÉGOCIANT À BEAUNE, COTE-D'OR, FRANCE

FRANCE

Starters

As a general rule, serve light before heavy, young before old, white before red. If you stick to these simple rules for serving wine, you won't go far wrong. The complications can come when you are trying to match the wine to food and make a balanced feast.

Starters should usually be light affairs that won't spoil your appetite — even the more robust dishes in this section should be served in small portions so they don't fill you up too much. The same is true of the wine to be drunk with them. The alternative is to drink the same wine throughout the meal. If you want to do this, choose a medium-bodied, all-rounder, such as an oaked Chardonnay or a light Pinot Noir. Finally, don't forget that Champagne can work well throughout a meal, from the aperitif onwards.

Strong flavours need strong wines, but remember that you are at the beginning of the meal and what you serve now may compromise the wine for the next course. Think of quantity as well as the style of wine — you don't want to overwhelm people with large amounts of wine when there are still two courses to come.

Montrachet 1996 Marquis de Laguiche Joseph Drouhin
This is a smooth, velvety wine, a perfect example of classic Burgundian treatment of the Chardonnay grape. It goes perfectly with fish, seafood and cream sauces.

Lyonnais Onion Soup

This is a filling soup, a delicious classic that is traditionally devoured after getting home very late from a night out. It's invigorating, warming and totally satisfying.

SERVES 8–10

60g butter
1 tbsp vegetable oil
1kg best-quality onions,
  peeled and sliced
1 bottle dry white wine
1 tbsp butter
60g plain flour
1.8 litres beef stock
5 egg yolks
100ml port
250g crème fraîche
1 baguette
300g Gruyère cheese,
  grated

Beef stock

2kg oxtails and beef
  rib bones
1 onion, peeled and
  roughly chopped
2 celery sticks, roughly
  chopped,
1 carrot, peeled and
  roughly chopped
sprig of thyme
bay leaf

Melt the 60g of butter and a tablespoon of oil in a pan over medium heat and add the sliced onions. Cook, stirring occasionally, until the onions caramelise and become sweet and tender – don't cover the pan. Once the onions are done, add the white wine and cook until reduced by half.

Melt the tablespoon of butter in a pan. Add the flour and mix well to make a roux. Cook until a light brown colour but take care not to let the mixture burn. Pour on the beef stock, whisking well, and simmer for 5 minutes. Add this mixture to the onions, season well and cook for a further 30 minutes.

Preheat the grill. Mix the egg yolks, port and crème fraîche together and divide equally between ovenproof soup bowls. Add the piping hot soup, stirring it into the egg mixture with a fork. Add some toasted croutons made from a baguette, generously sprinkle with Gruyère cheese and glaze under a hot grill until the cheese is golden and bubbling. Serve immediately

Beef stock Roast the bones in a hot oven (220°C/gas 7) with the vegetables and herbs until brown all over. Remove the bones from the roasting tin and put in a pan on top of the stove. Cover with water, bring to the boil and skim. Simmer for 1½ hours, then strain.

WINES

If you have to have something to drink, sip a sherry or a drop of Pinot Gris, which goes well with the sweetness of the onions. If you really want to go native, leave about two tablespoons of soup in the bottom of your bowl. Pour in a splash of ordinary red wine, such as a Côtes du Rhône, add a little dry bread and slurp!

MANZANILLA SHERRY
ALSACE PINOT GRIS
CÔTES DU RHÔNE RED

Cold Mushroom Soup with Black Olive Cream

Accompanied by some warm crusty bread, this is a perfect summer starter. The mushrooms give it an almost meaty taste. Be sure to serve the soup really cold.

SERVES 6

360g wild mushrooms, such as field, bolet and chanterelle
1 tbsp butter
600ml white chicken stock
salt and pepper
juice of 2 lemons
180ml whipping cream
2 tbsp black olive paste (tapenade)
a handful of basil, chervil and chives, roughly chopped
cayenne pepper

White chicken stock
(makes about 2 litres)
1kg chicken bones or wing tips
1 calf's foot, split
1 onion
1 small leek
2 sticks of celery
2 sprigs of thyme
6 parsley stalks

Clean the mushrooms, but avoid washing them unless it's really necessary. Cut them into big cubes, put in a saucepan with the butter and cook over a medium heat for 5 minutes. The mushrooms should give off some moisture and become soft.

Add the stock, season with salt and pepper and bring to a gentle boil. Add the lemon juice after 5 minutes. Blend the soup until smooth, pass through a sieve, cover and chill.

Whisk the cream until it forms peaks and fold in the olive paste. Divide the soup between the bowls and gently add the olive paste mixture to form a frothy cream top. Sprinkle over the herbs and a pinch of cayenne pepper.

White chicken stock Place the bones and calf's foot in a large pan, cover with 2.5 litres of water and bring to the boil. Skim off any fat and scum that come to the surface. Turn the heat down, add the rest of the ingredients and simmer for 1½ hours, skimming occasionally. Pass through a fine sieve and leave to cool. This stock can be kept in the refrigerator for up to 5 days or frozen.

WINES

Rosé d'Anjou used to be a quite sickly wine, but has now become very palatable, especially with mushroom dishes. If you prefer to drink a red, a young Merlot is the best choice.

ROSÉ D'ANJOU
YOUNG CALIFORNIA MERLOT

Cold Tomato and Orange Soup

This is a drink as much as a soup. Serve chilled, even on the rocks, and with a splash of vodka if you like. The tomatoes must be very ripe and sweet.

Remove the eyes of the tomatoes and cut into halves. Place in a blender with the orange juice, sugar, coriander seeds, tomato paste, salt and Tabasco and blitz until smooth. Press the soup through a fine sieve and chill. Drizzle with a little olive oil before serving and accompany with some toasted slices of baguette and either chorizo or lomo sausage. Add the splash of vodka just before serving.

WINES
If you are adding vodka to the soup, serve nothing else to drink. Otherwise, if you're serving chorizo or lomo alongside, a fino sherry with its dry finish is a perfect match. Failing that, New Zealand Sauvignon Blanc is a very tomato-friendly wine.

FINO SHERRY
NEW ZEALAND SAUVIGNON BLANC

SERVES 6
12 large, ripe plum
   tomatoes
250ml fresh orange juice
1 tbsp caster sugar
1 tbsp coriander seeds
2 tbsp tomato paste
salt and Tabasco to taste
extra-virgin olive oil
baguette, sliced and toasted
chorizo or lomo
vodka (optional)

Duck and Vermicelli Soup flavoured with Lemon Grass

With its strong Asian flavours, this is one of my favourite soups. You can add some seafood, such as lobster or prawns, if you wish.

SERVES 8

4 turnips, peeled
4 courgettes
1 small leek
2 large duck legs,
  about 400g
2 sticks of celery
1 onion, cut into quarters
8 star anise
1tbsp demerara sugar
salt and pepper
1 stick lemon grass
small piece lime peel
160g Chinese rice
  vermicelli, pre-cooked
4 spring onions, thinly
  sliced
sesame oil
1 bunch of fresh coriander
juice of 1 lime

Cut the turnips into fine julienne strips. Save the trimmings for later. Wash the courgettes and cut into julienne like the turnip – avoid the cores which may be a little soft. Prepare the leek in the same way, again keeping the trimmings. Blanch the vegetables in boiling water for a very short time and refresh in iced water – they should still be crunchy. Drain and set aside.

Put the duck legs into a pot with the celery, onion, trimmings from the turnip and leek, star anise, sugar, salt and pepper. Cover with a generous amount of water (about 2 litres), bring to a gentle simmer and skim well. Remove the outer part and top of the lemon grass and add to the pot along with the lime peel. Simmer for 1 hour, then leave to cool for 30 minutes.

Remove the duck legs and shred the meat, discarding the skin and bones. Pass the liquid through a fine sieve, check the seasoning and bring to the boil. Add the pre-cooked vermicelli, duck meat, blanched vegetables and thinly sliced spring onions. Finely chop the inner part of the lemon grass and add to the pot. Finish with a drizzle of sesame oil, chopped coriander leaves and lime juice.

WINES

Australian Riesling, with its density and slightly oily feel, always goes well with Asian-style food. Although this is a soup, it has plenty to chew on and could be accompanied by an Alsace Pinot Noir. Alternatively, there is always sherry – the classic soup drink.

AUSTRALIAN RIESLING
ALSACE PINOT NOIR
AMONTILLADO SHERRY

Velouté de Coquillages au Champagne Parfumé à la Muscade

Creamy and rich, but light, this is a favourite of Le Gavroche customers. The flavours are intense and there is enough texture to warrant a wine.

Wash the mussels, cockles and clams in cold water. Trim and clean the squid, removing the 'beak' inside. Slice the body into rounds and keep the bunches of tentacles whole. Peel the langoustines and discard the shells.

Put the clams and mussels in separate pans over high heat and divide the wine equally between them. Cover and leave to cook for 4–6 minutes depending on the size of the shellfish. Be careful not to overcook them or they will go chewy. Drain and keep the juice.

Pick out the meat from the clams and mussels and place in soup bowls or a tureen. Add the rest of the seafood. Strain the juice through a fine sieve and put into a pan over a high heat. When it boils, add the double cream and crème fraîche. Bring back to the boil again, season well and add the lemon juice. Pour this piping hot mixture over the seafood. Grate a little nutmeg on top and serve immediately. The soup can be frothed with a hand blender.

WINES

When in doubt, drink Champagne. Ultra Brut is very dry but marries beautifully with seafood. A grand Chablis goes well with the creaminess of this soup, or try an Alsace Riesling, which complements the nutmeg flavour.

CHAMPAGNE ULTRA BRUT
CHABLIS GRAND CRU
ALSACE RIESLING

SERVES 6
500g mussels
500g cockles
500g surf clams, or any
   small clams
6 baby squid
6 cooked langoustines
1 bottle dry Champagne or
   white wine
100g cooked peeled brown
   shrimps
300ml double cream
250g crème fraîche
juice of 2 lemons
salt, pepper, nutmeg

Oxtail Broth with Pearl Barley

This is a very thick wintry soup — a hearty first course or a good lunch dish. And a Thermos flask full of this warming broth makes a very welcome snack on a bracing Highlands walk.

SERVES 6

1 large oxtail, about 1.6kg
2 sticks of celery
1 carrot, peeled
2 garlic cloves, peeled
1 sprig of thyme
1 clove
2 bay leaves
1 onion
vegetable oil
salt and pepper
180g pearl barley
Worcestershire sauce

Garnish

2 carrots, peeled and diced
1 leek, washed and sliced in
   half lengthways and then
   across

Take the oxtail and section it through the joints. Place the pieces in a very large cast-iron pot and cover generously with water (about 3 litres). Add the celery, carrot, garlic, thyme, clove and bay leaves.

Cut the onion in half, but do not peel. Brush the cut side with oil and place it cut side down on a hot plate or griddle. Leave until burnt, caramelised and very dark brown, then add to the pot. This gives flavour and colour. Bring the soup to the boil, skim and then turn down the heat to a very gentle simmer. Season lightly with salt and pepper. The oxtail should take 2½–3 hours to cook, depending on its thickness. The meat should be tender and come off the bone easily.

Once the oxtail is cooked, take the pot off the heat and leave to cool. When warm enough to handle, strain the cooking liquid through a fine sieve into a clean pot. Add the barley and the garnish vegetables and simmer for a further 35–40 minutes. Meanwhile, pick the meat off the oxtail and keep warm. Pour the boiling hot broth and barley on to the meat and add a few dashes of Worcestershire sauce.

WINES

Sherry is always a good choice for drinking with soup and an Amontillado or an old Madeira can match the strong flavours in this broth. An Australian Syrah would be a good alternative.

AMONTILLADO SHERRY
OLD VINTAGE MADEIRA
AUSTRALIAN SYRAH

Garbure Béarnaise

This soup is from Southwest France. Hearty and filling, it can be served as a main course as well as in small portions as a starter.

Soak the beans in cold water for two hours. Trim and wash the cabbage, cut it into four and slice thinly. Blanch the slices in boiling water until cooked but still a little crisp, then refresh in iced water. Drain and set aside.

Heat the duck fat in a large saucepan. Cut the duck or goose necks into 4cm rounds and fry in the duck fat. Once the meat is golden, add the peeled, sliced onions and garlic and continue to cook, stirring occasionally. After 5 minutes, add 2 litres of water, the drained beans, thyme, hock and belly pork and bring to a very gentle simmer. Skim. Partially cover with a lid and continue to cook for about 2 hours or until the meat is tender. Add the carrots and potatoes and cook for another 30 minutes.

Take out the meat and roughly break it up. Put it back in the soup with the shredded duck confit and blanched cabbage. Season and serve piping hot with grilled sourdough bread.

WINES
Cahors, a wine from the same region as this recipe, is the ideal drink. A Malbec also has strong enough flavours to match this robust soup.

RED CAHORS
YOUNG ARGENTINIAN MALBEC

SERVES 8
100g dry white beans
  (Lingots or Coco)
1 savoy cabbage
100g duck or goose fat
2 duck or goose necks,
  skin off
300g onions, peeled and
  sliced
3 garlic cloves, peeled and
  sliced
2 sprigs of thyme
1 green (unsmoked) hock
400g salted belly pork
400g carrots, peeled and
  diced
400g potatoes (Charlotte,
  Belle de Fontenay),
  peeled and diced
2 duck legs confit, shredded
salt and pepper

Moules Marinière

This classic dish never fails to be greeted by 'oohs' and 'aahs', but is simple to make. Served piping hot, it is a real treat. Don't forget to provide spoons for the broth at the end.

SERVES 4

3kg mussels

1 large onion, peeled and finely chopped

4 sticks of celery, finely chopped

1 garlic clove, peeled and finely chopped

1 tbsp butter

400ml dry white wine

200g crème fraîche

1 bunch of flat-leaf parsley, chopped

salt and pepper

Wash and scrape the mussels, discarding any broken ones. Sweat the chopped onion, celery and garlic with the butter in a large, tall saucepan. Pour in the wine and bring to a rapid boil. Add the mussels and cover. After 3 minutes shake the pan and stir the mussels. Cover again and continue to cook until all the mussels have opened, about 7 or 8 minutes. Discard any that haven't opened by this time.

Remove the mussels with a slotted spoon and put them in a big tureen or individual deep bowls. Continue to boil the liquid in the pan. Add the crème fraîche, parsley and seasoning, and as soon as the liquid has come back to the boil, pour it over the mussels. Serve at once.

WINES

Muscadet would be my first choice for this dish, but German Weisse beers or a Bière de Garde, such as La Choulette, also work well with mussels and other seafood.

MUSCADET

GERMAN WEISSE BEER

BIÈRE DE GARDE

Rare Peppered Tuna with Ginger and Sesame Dressing

With its meaty flavours and tangy vinaigrette, this dish is my daughter Emily's favourite. Soy and chilli are not wine friendly, but who says the wine should always take priority?

SERVES 6

480g tuna loin, preferably
  yellowfin
1 tbsp black and white
  peppercorns, crushed
2 tbsp sesame seeds
6cm piece of fresh ginger
1 medium-hot red chilli
1 tbsp clear honey
6 tbsp Japanese soy sauce
juice of 2 limes
2 tbsp sesame oil
2 spring onions, thinly
  sliced

Take the tuna and remove any dark areas in the middle. Cut into manageable strips about 4cm wide. Roll these in the crushed pepper, pressing them slightly so the pepper holds. Sear the tuna strips on a grill or a non-stick pan on all sides, but don't cook for more than 4 minutes. It must stay very rare. Put the tuna aside to cool slightly, then cut into thin slices, 5mm thick, and place on a serving dish.

To make the sauce, first toast the sesame seeds in a dry pan until lightly golden. Peel the ginger and cut into very fine julienne strips. Slice the chilli – discard the seeds if you don't want the dish to be very hot. Mix together the honey, soy sauce, lime juice and sesame oil with a fork. Add the sesame seeds, spring onion, ginger and chilli and serve with the tuna.

WINES

There's a lot going on here, which is why the Chardonnay Verdelo blend, with its full-on richness, is a good choice. A Viognier blend from Côtes du Rhône would also suit, or how about a good quality saké (when in Rome…) or even a fruity Lambic Belgian beer?

AUSTRALIAN CHARDONNAY (VERDELO)
WHITE CÔTES DU RHÔNE (VIOGNIER)
SAKÉ
BELGIAN FRUIT BEER

Salad Monte-Cristo

The lobster should not be chilled, and it's even better served warm. Likewise the eggs. This old-fashioned lobster salad takes some beating for flavour and texture. Great for a picnic or supper at Glyndebourne.

To kill the lobsters humanely, pierce the head in between the eyes with a heavy knife. Plunge the lobsters into boiling water and cook for 8 minutes. Leave to cool. Crack the lobsters open, pick out all the meat and cut it up into bite-size pieces. Peel the eggs, chop them roughly and add to the lobster.

Wash the potatoes and cook in salted water. Leave to cool, then peel and cut into the same size pieces as the lobsters. Gently fold them into the lobster mix. Whisk the cream and mustard into the mayonnaise. Place some lobster mix into each lettuce heart, then spoon over the mayonnaise dressing. Sprinkle with snipped tarragon leaves.

WINES

Soave from the Verona region of Italy has a mouth-filling texture and a heady scent that at its best is quite exceptional. Pinot Grigio would be a good option if you prefer something lighter, or go for the always reliable bubbly.

DRY SOAVE
PINOT GRIGIO
NON-VINTAGE CHAMPAGNE

SERVES 6
2 lobsters, 500g each
6 hard-boiled eggs
600g salad potatoes
   (Charlotte, Belle de
   Fontenay)
4 tbsp single cream
4 tbsp wholegrain mustard
4 tbsp mayonnaise
6 lettuce hearts
tarragon leaves

Spicy Crab and Glass Noodle Salad

This is so easy even my wife Gisele manages to make it well. And she swears the idea was hers!

SERVES 4
160g glass noodles
4cm piece fresh ginger
1 red onion, peeled and
  thinly sliced
1 red chilli, thinly sliced
1 garlic clove, finely
  chopped
1 tbsp crunchy peanut
  butter
2 tbsp fish sauce
1 tbsp light muscovado
  sugar
4 tbsp blended sesame oil
juice of 4 limes
salt and pepper
1 bunch of fresh coriander
200g picked fresh crab claw
  meat

Pour boiling water over the noodles to cook as the instructions on the packet, usually 3 minutes, then drain. Peel the ginger and cut into very thin julienne strips. Toss the ginger, onion and chilli with the noodles.

Make a vinaigrette with the garlic, peanut butter, fish sauce, sugar, oil, lime juice, salt and pepper. Dress the salad with this, sprinkle the crabmeat on top and garnish with sprigs of coriander.

WINES

A lightly oaked Sauvignon Blanc from the Loire Valley, such as Pouilly Fumé, has enough acidity to stand up to this lively salad. Likewise, the ever-improving English sparkling wine would be quite at home. In Singapore and Hong Kong many people drink spirits with food, but this is not for me unless watered down.

POUILLY FUMÉ
ENGLISH SPARKLING WHITE
BLENDED WHISKY

Creamy Crab Gratin

Serve these little pots with toasted sourdough bread as a starter or make in a large dish as a rather rich and luxurious main course.

SERVES 4
400g picked crab meat
  (claw meat only)
4 shallots, finely chopped
4 tbsp port
2 egg yolks
salt, pepper, nutmeg
120ml crème fraîche
50g Parmesan cheese,
  grated

Gently mix the crab with all the other ingredients except the Parmesan. Divide into 4 ovenproof ramekin dishes or similar. Sprinkle the Parmesan on top and bake in a preheated oven, 180°C/gas 4, for 8–10 minutes. If the cheese has not browned, place the dishes under a hot grill for a few seconds.

WINES

WHITE CHÂTEAUNEUF DU PAPE
MACON VILLAGES

Skate Ravioli

A different and easy way to use skate. This pasta dough is made with the whites of the eggs only and is very tender. You'll need a round, fluted cutter, about 5cm in diameter, to cut out the ravioli.

SERVES 8

Pasta dough
500g plain flour
pinch of salt
200g egg whites

Skate
4 small skate wings, about
    1.6kg in all
salt and pepper
1 celery heart, use just the
    yellow core with the
    leaves
2 tbsp baby capers in
    vinegar
2 lemons, skin and pith
    removed and divided into
    segments
1 tbsp flat-leaf parsley,
    washed and roughly
    chopped
1 tbsp curly parsley, washed
    and roughly chopped

Beurre blanc
4 shallots, peeled and
    finely chopped
200ml dry white wine
90ml double cream
250g unsalted butter, cut
    into small dice
salt and white pepper

Pasta dough Knead the flour, salt and egg whites together to form an elastic but not sticky dough, adding water if needed. Wrap in clingfilm and leave in the refrigerator to rest for at least an hour.

Skate Skin the skate and remove the flesh from the bone. With a large knife, shred the skate into thin strips no more than 5mm thick. Season well, then add the chopped celery heart and leaves.

Roll out the pasta dough on a pasta machine as thinly as possible. Divide the skate mix into 24 balls and place them on the sheets of pasta, making sure there is plenty of space around each one – it's a good idea to mark out the areas with the cutter first. Brush round the balls with water to moisten, then place another sheet of pasta on top. Press down well all round the balls to shape the ravioli, then cut them out with the fluted cutter. Take each one in your hand and press down the edges to extract any air inside and seal the edges properly, then cut again. Bring a big pan of salted water to the boil. Add the ravioli and cook for 6–8 minutes. Serve hot with the beurre blanc, adding the capers, lemon segments and chopped parsley.

Beurre blanc Put the shallots and white wine in a pan to simmer. When the wine has reduced by half, add the cream and boil for 1 minute. Whisk in the butter a little at a time, over a medium heat. When all the butter is whisked in, take off the heat and season.

WINES

For this dish you need a wine that can cope with the acidity of the lemon and capers. Muscadet and Sancerre are obvious choices. Verdicchio, a less well-known wine from central Italy, has a fuller flavour with a light sparkle.

MUSCADET
SANCERRE
VERDICCHIO

Tiger Prawn and Apple Salad

Use fresh tiger prawns, rather than frozen, if you can, or you could make this dish with languoustines. This is a popular salad at Le Gavroche des Tropiques in Mauritius.

Shell and de-vein the prawns. Smear them with a little oil and season, then cook briefly on a hot grill until pink but still juicy.

To make the dressing, crush the garlic in a mortar or blender and mix to a paste with the rest of the oil and the honey and curry powder. Add the lime juice and half of the lemon juice.

Cut the apples into matchstick-size pieces and place in cold water with the remaining lemon juice to keep them white. Cut the lettuce into manageable pieces and the chives into matchsticks. Toss the apples, lettuce and chives in the dressing. Season well and serve with the prawns on top.

WINES
Naturally dry German Riesling offers a good balance with seafood and goes well with the oriental tang of this salad. The Sauvignon Blanc from Chile is not only good value but full and fragrant in flavour. Wines from the Casablanca region are especially good. White Portuguese Vinho Verde is always interesting and good with spice, garlic and seafood, but should always be drunk within 12 months of being bottled.

GERMAN RIESLING KABINETT
CHILEAN SAUVIGNON BLANC
VINHO VERDE

SERVES 6
18 tiger prawns
6 tbsp vegetable oil
2 garlic cloves
2 tsp clear honey
1 tsp Madras curry powder
juice of 2 limes
juice of 1 lemon
2 Granny Smith apples
3 little gem lettuce
1 bunch of chives
salt and pepper

Aïoli of Vegetables, Whelks and Razor Clams

This is Provençal cooking at its best — simple, gutsy food that is meant to be enjoyed outside in the sunshine with friends.

SERVES 8
200g small carrots
400g small courgettes
300g French beans
200g cauliflower
250g baby fennel
500g new potatoes
400g whelks
800g razor clams

Aïoli
10 garlic cloves, peeled
2 egg yolks
1 tbsp Dijon mustard
juice of 1 lemon
320ml olive oil
salt and pepper

Peel the carrots and wash and trim the courgettes, beans, cauliflower and fennel. Divide the cauliflower into florets and leave the rest of the vegetables whole. Blanch in boiling salted water until just cooked, then refresh in iced water to halt the cooking and keep their vibrant colour. Drain and set aside.

Peel the potatoes and boil in salted water until fully cooked. Keep warm in the water. Boil the whelks in heavily salted water for 20 minutes, then drop in the razor clams and cook for 2–3 minutes more. Drain and serve immediately.

Re-heat the vegetables in a steamer or in boiling water. Arrange them on a large platter with the seafood in the middle and serve warm, with the aïoli in a separate bowl.

Aïoli Put the garlic cloves, egg yolks, mustard and lemon juice in a food processor. Blitz while drizzling in the olive oil until the mixture is thick with the texture of mayonnaise. This can be done with a pestle and mortar, but the food processor does a very good job as long as you don't over-blitz the mixture. Season to taste.

WINES
The little coastal town of Bandol, near Toulon, is better known for its red wines, but also produces rich, mouth-filling rosés with just enough acidity for this Provençal speciality. Further up the coast is Cassis, where the white wines are equally refreshing. The Macon Blanc will also satisfy, but has a little less acidity.

BANDOL ROSÉ
WHITE CASSIS
MACON BLANC

Freshwater Crayfish with Vin Jaune

*A seriously refined and elegant dish, worth every second it takes to prepare.
Vin Jaune is a very unusual wine made in the Jura region of France. It is
similar to sherry in taste, but a good one such as Château Chalon is far
more complex than a sherry. The wine is aged in barrels with a natural
yeast cover for a minimum of six years. The yeast and gradual oxidisation
give taste and depth and makes this one of the great wines of the world.*

Rinse the crayfish under a cold tap. Remove the intestines by pulling
on the centre part of the tail. Plunge the crayfish immediately into
salted boiling water, cook for 4 minutes, then drain. Crack them
open and shell, keeping six whole for decoration and reserving the
heads for later. Soak the morels in just enough water to cover. When
they are soft, drain and pass the soaking liquid through a muslin cloth.
Boil the liquid until reduced by half. Cut the morels into slices and
wash them well.

Heat 1 tablespoon of butter and a little oil in a large pan and sweat
4 peeled, chopped shallots. Add the crayfish heads and crush with the
end of a rolling pin. Turn up the heat and stir for 5–6 minutes. Add
the wine, boil for 5–6 minutes longer, then add the morel juice and
cream and simmer for 20 minutes. Season well and pass the liquid
through a fine sieve, pressing well to extract as much juice as possible.

In another pan sweat the remaining peeled, chopped shallots and
butter with the morels for 10 minutes until soft. Add these to the
sauce and bring to the boil. Place the crayfish in the pan and remove
from the heat – the sauce should be hot enough to warm the crayfish
without making them tough. Serve immediately.

WINES
The combination of musky mushrooms and cream with crayfish is
hard to beat. This dish deserves a grand wine and they don't come any
grander than Montrachet, a strong, dry, yet gorgeously rounded, white
wine from Burgundy. An Australian Chardonnay is a good alternative.

CHÂTEAU CHALON
MONTRACHET
ADELAIDE HILLS CHARDONNAY

SERVES 6
35 freshwater crayfish
80g dried morel
   mushrooms
2 tbsp butter
olive oil
6 shallots
200ml Vin Jaune
300ml double cream
200ml crème fraîche
salt and pepper

Tartare of Sea Bass with Dill

The perfect starter — fresh zingy flavours that only sea bass has, embellished with a little caviar. Needless to say, the sea bass must be perfectly fresh and it's best to use larger fish as the texture is better.

SERVES 6

500g sea bass fillets

2 shallots, peeled and finely chopped

1 small bunch of fresh dill, chopped

3 tbsp full-fat Greek yoghurt

juice of 1 lime

green Tabasco to taste

salt

caviar (optional)

This dish must not be dressed until the very last minute otherwise the fish will burn from the seasoning and the texture will change.

Rinse the fish and remove all bones and skin. Dice the flesh and put in a bowl set on ice.

Add the chopped shallots to the fish with the chopped dill. Fold in the yoghurt and lime juice, and season with Tabasco and salt to taste. I prefer to use green Tabasco for this recipe as it is fragrant and not quite so strong.

Serve with hot toasted brown bread and a salad of little gem lettuce leaves dressed with nut oil and lemon juice. If you're feeling extravagant, add a generous spoonful of caviar to each serving!

WINES

Chardonnay-blend Champagne works well with the creaminess of this fresh, light starter, with or without the caviar. If you don't want bubbles, an Australian Margaret River Chardonnay has a rounded palate with enough acidity. A good young Chablis is another option.

GOOD FULL-BODIED CHAMPAGNE

AUSTRALIAN MARGARET RIVER CHARDONNAY

YOUNG CHABLIS

Smoked Eel with Beetroot and Horseradish Cream

Tried and tested, perfect combinations like this cannot be bettered.
Use fresh horseradish if you can get it, but beware — it is much stronger
than the bottled relish.

SERVES 6

1 smoked eel, about 1.2kg

250ml whipping cream

4 tbsp horseradish relish

1 tsp English mustard

600g raw firm medium-size
  beetroot

1 tbsp olive oil

salt and pepper

3 tbsp red wine vinegar

1 bunch of flat-leaf parsley,
  chopped

3 shallots, peeled and finely
  chopped

If using a whole smoked eel, remove the skin and head, then cut straight down the eel from top to tail to remove the main bone. With a sharp, thin-bladed knife, run down the sides to remove the smaller bones. You can buy pre-filleted eel, but a whole fish will provide more moist fillets. Cut the flesh into diamonds about 5cm long and set aside.

Whisk the cream until stiff, then fold in the horseradish and mustard. Peel the beetroot and cut into small wedges. Put these in a non-stick pan with a tablespoon of olive oil, season and cover loosely with greaseproof paper. Fry gently, tossing the pan occasionally, and continue to cook very slowly until the beetroot are tender and sweet. Pour in the vinegar, chopped parsley and shallots. Arrange the warm beetroot on the plate, lay the eel on top and add a generous spoonful of the horseradish cream

WINES

The sharpness of the Aligoté and the bold pungency of the Savennières are what's needed with the fatty smoked eel. Ice-cold Aquavit would also make an interesting way to start the meal, as long as you don't overdo it!

BOURGOGNE ALIGOTÉ

SAVENNIÈRES (ANJOU) 6–10 YEARS OLD

AQUAVIT

Melon with Parma Ham

This is a classic combination that is quite simply irresistible if the melons are ripe and the ham of good quality. On no account use the stuff that's like pre-sliced cardboard for this dish.

SERVES 4

2 perfectly ripe Charentais
   or rock melons
16 slices Parma ham, or if
   feeling extravagant a
   Spanish jamón such as
   38-month old Iberico or
   Serrano
freshly ground white
   pepper

Cut the melon into segments and remove the skin and seeds. Drape the slices of ham round the melon and liberally sprinkle with freshly ground white pepper. Don't serve too cold or the scent of the melon will be masked.

WINES

A Charentais melon with wine from the Charente region is ideal. Pineau, a fortified wine, works well with the fruitiness of the melon and the saltiness of the ham. A medium Oloroso sherry or even a Bual Madeira would be almost as good.

RED PINEAU DES CHARENTES
MEDIUM OLOROSO SHERRY
BUAL MADEIRA

Cardoon Gratin with Marrow

Peel off the outer stalks of the cardoon, like you would a celery, and cut into quarters. Place in a pan of cold, salted water with the lemon juice. Bring to the boil and simmer for 20–30 minutes until tender. Leave to cool, then drain.

Soak the marrow bones in cold, salted water for 1 hour. Push out the marrow, cut into 1cm slices and gently poach in salted, simmering water for 30 seconds. Drain and set aside.

Boil the stock until it is reduced by half and syrupy. Add the shallots and garlic to the breadcrumbs, cheese and parsley with a little seasoning. Cut the cardoon quarters into manageable pieces about 5–6cm long and pan fry in a non-stick pan with a little olive oil until golden brown. Place these into gratin dishes. Spoon over the reduced stock, then the poached marrow and top with the crumb mix. Bake in a preheated oven, 200°C/gas 6, for 8 minutes and serve immediately. If necessary, place the dish under a grill to colour and crisp the crumb mix.

Veal stock Roast the bones and calf's foot in a hot oven, 220°C/gas 7, until brown, turning occasionally. Transfer to a large saucepan. Put the vegetables in the roasting pan and roast until golden, turning frequently. Pour off any excess fat and add to the pot with the bones. Put the roasting pan over a high heat and deglaze with 500ml of water to loosen the caramelised roasting sugars. Pour into the pan. Add the rest of the ingredients and 4.5 litres of water and bring to the boil. Simmer for 3 hours, skimming occasionally. Pass through a fine sieve and leave to cool. This makes about 3.5 litres but can be frozen.

WINES
This is a vegetable dish masquerading as meat, hence the Syrah rosé, which has a full-on fruit flavour, almost like a red wine. Alternatively, try a light red such as a Pinot Noir from the Alsace region. Zinfandel is a very versatile wine that goes with most vegetable-based dishes.

PROVENCE SYRAH ROSÉ
ALSACE PINOT NOIR
CALIFORNIA ZINFANDEL

SERVES 6
1 cardoon
juice of 2 lemons
2kg centre-cut veal/beef
  marrow bones
500ml veal stock
2 shallots, peeled and finely
  chopped
2 garlic cloves, peeled and
  finely chopped
150g dry breadcrumbs
1 tbsp grated Parmesan
  cheese
2 tbsp chopped parsley
salt and pepper
olive oil

Veal stock
1.5kg veal knuckle bones,
  chopped
1 calf's foot, split
1 large onion, chopped
2 large carrots, chopped
1 stick of celery, chopped
2 garlic cloves
2 sprigs of thyme
½ tbsp tomato purée

Chicken Satay

What more can I say about these tasty morsels? They're often badly done, but when they're good it's difficult to stop eating them. You'll need some bamboo skewers for this dish.

SERVES 6

4cm fresh root ginger

20ml vegetable or
  groundnut oil

100ml pineapple juice,
  preferably fresh

2 tbsp sesame oil

2 tbsp dark soy sauce

2 tbsp light muscovado
  sugar

2 tbsp rice vinegar or sherry
  vinegar

2 garlic cloves, crushed

8 large chicken thighs

Peanut sauce

250g crunchy peanut
  butter

1 tbsp light muscovado
  sugar

1 tbsp dark soy sauce

juice and zest of 2 limes

Tabasco to taste

Peel and grate or very finely chop the ginger. Mix the ginger with the rest of the ingredients – except the chicken. Remove the skin and bone from the chicken thighs and slice into strips about 2.5cm wide. Soak the bamboo skewers in water for 20 minutes before skewering the pieces of chicken. Dip each skewer of chicken into the marinade and gently rub it in. Set aside for at least an hour. Grill on a barbecue over medium heat until cooked through. Serve with peanut sauce.

Peanut sauce Dissolve the peanut butter and sugar in 200ml of warm water. Add the rest of the ingredients and mix well.

WINES

It's hard to find a wine to match with peanuts, but a good chilled white lager always works well. Another way to approach the problem is by going for sweetness and power and an old highly scented Riesling would be good. If you want to drink red, a strong, plummy Australian Shiraz would be my choice.

WHITE LAGER

FLOWERY OLD RIESLING

STRONG AUSTRALIAN SHIRAZ

Roast Chicken Salad

SERVES 8

1 leek, trimmed, washed and sliced thinly

1 small corn-fed chicken, about 1.3kg

salt and pepper

olive oil for roasting the chicken

4 shallots, peeled and chopped

5 tbsp extra virgin strong olive oil

125ml dry white wine

3 tbsp balsamic vinegar

1 tbsp honey

1 tbsp wholegrain mustard

2 globe artichokes, trimmed to reveal the heart and chokes removed

500g mixed salad leaves, such as mizuna, wild rocket, cress or baby spinach

a small baguette cut into 24 thin slices

1 garlic clove

Blanch the leek slices in boiling salted water for 30 seconds and refresh in iced water. Leave to drain. Rub the chicken with salt, pepper and a little olive oil and roast in a preheated oven, 190°C/gas 5, for 45 minutes until golden and cooked through. Remove the chicken from the roasting pan and leave to rest in a warm place.

Drain off some of the fat from the pan and add the shallots with 1 tablespoon of fresh olive oil. Cook for 2–3 minutes, stirring well. Add the wine, reduce by half and add any juices from the chicken. Take off the heat and whisk in the vinegar, honey, mustard and 4 tablespoons of olive oil. Cut the trimmed artichokes into segments and pan fry in a non-stick pan with a little olive oil until browned. Add the leeks to warm them through and season well.

To serve, shred the chicken into bite-size pieces while still warm. Toss the warm leeks and artichokes in a little of the vinaigrette and arrange on the plates. Toss the leaves and finally the chicken. Garnish with fried croutons of baguette rubbed with the garlic clove.

WINES

Lightly-chilled Beaujolais or red Sancerre are good options, or a Valpolicella from the Verona region.

BEAUJOLAIS

SANCERRE RED

VALPOLICELLA

Mushroom Salad with Smoked Bacon and Sweet Mustard Dressing

The smell of bacon cooking is enough to give anyone hunger pangs.
A delicious salad.

Wash the salad and spin to dry. Boil the bacon for 10 minutes and leave to cool. Trim off the edges and cut into small matchsticks. Pan fry in a non-stick pan until golden and set aside. Pick over the black mushrooms, and wash them well. Blanch in boiling water for 15 seconds, refresh and drain. Place the black mushrooms and chopped shallots in a very hot non-stick pan with a drizzle of olive oil. Season and cook until golden, then add the bacon matchsticks.

Whisk all the dressing ingredients together and season. Put the cooked mushrooms, shallots and bacon into a large salad bowl with the raw mushrooms and mizuna salad leaves. Add the dressing and toss. Grill the streaky bacon slices until crispy and decorate the salad. Serve immediately.

WINES
Three very different beverages for the same salad, but they suit different occasions. Serve beer when the lads are round, rosé at a picnic or the Valpolicella at a dinner party.

BROWN ALE
ROSÉ DE PROVENCE
VALPOLICELLA

SERVES 6
300g mizuna salad leaves
300g piece of smoked streaky bacon (Alsace style)
120g black trumpet mushrooms
3 shallots, peeled and sliced
olive oil
250g firm white button mushrooms, sliced
6 very thin slices smoked streaky bacon

Dressing
1 tbsp wholegrain mustard
1 tbsp clear honey
2 tbsp red wine vinegar
3 tbsp olive oil
salt and pepper

Savoie Salad

Classic combinations like this are hard to beat. Increase the ingredients and this could make a light lunch as well as a starter.

SERVES 6

6 salad potatoes (Charlotte or Belle de Fontenay)

walnut oil

200g air-dried, lightly smoked bacon cut into lardons – 2 x 0.5cm

olive oil

red wine vinegar

750g mâche salad leaves (lamb's lettuce)

salt and pepper

2 shallots, peeled and thinly sliced

300g Comte, Gruyère or Beaufort cheese

Cook the washed potatoes in salted, boiling water. When they are cool enough to handle, peel and slice thinly. Drizzle the slices with little walnut oil, season, then cover and keep warm.

Gently fry the lardons in a pan with a smear of olive oil – the lardons should be crispy but not dry. Sprinkle in a few drops of vinegar and add all of this to the potatoes.

Dress the well-washed salad with a little walnut oil, vinegar, salt and pepper. Add the shallots and then the warm potato mix. Finally, sprinkle over shavings of the cheese. Serve warm.

WINES

The obvious partner for this salad is the Rousette, with its pleasant grassy, lemony taste – also delicious as an aperitif. Other choices are a light red, such as the ever-improving Gamay from Ardèche, or a typical Pinot Noir from Switzerland.

ROUSETTE DE SAVOIE

ARDÈCHE GAMAY

SWISS NEUCHÂTEL PINOT NOIR

Pig's Head Brawn

If possible, buy Middle White or Tamworth pork for this recipe as the flavour will be far more piggy than ordinary pork.

SERVES 12

1 boned pig's head, with
 tongue but not brain
500g coarse sea salt
1 tbsp cracked white/black
 peppercorns
1 tbsp caster sugar
1 sprig of thyme
1 tsp saltpetre
1 bouquet garni of thyme,
 bay, parsley stalks, leek
2 garlic cloves, peeled
2 carrots, peeled
2 sticks of celery, cut into
 chunks
1 leek, cut into chunks
1 large onion, peeled and
 cut into chunks
1 bottle dry white wine
4 shallots, peeled and
 chopped
2 sprigs curly parsley,
 chopped
2 tbsp wholegrain mustard
salt and pepper

Ask your butcher to bone out the head and singe the down and hairs. It then has to be scraped with a sharp knife to remove any bristle that is left. Rinse the tongue and dry well. Mix together the sea salt, cracked pepper, sugar, thyme and saltpetre with your hands. Rub this mixture on to the head and tongue and lay flat in a plastic or stainless steel dish with the remaining salt mix over it. Cover with clingfilm and refrigerate for 10 days. Turn the meat over after 5 days.

After 10 days, rinse the head under cold running water for 5 minutes. Put it in a large saucepan, cover with water and add the bouquet garni, garlic, peeled whole carrots, celery, leek, onion and half the wine. Simmer for 35–40 minutes. Skim well, then remove the tongue and peel off the skin. Place the tongue back in the pan and continue to simmer gently until the meat is tender, about 3 hours. Top up with hot water when necessary.

Remove the head and pass the cooking liquid through a fine sieve. Set the liquid aside, keep the carrots and discard the rest of the vegetables. Cut the carrots into 1cm dice and set aside. Cut the head, ears and tongue into 2cm dice. The skin should be tender and gelatinous and any fat should also be diced up. Put the chopped shallots in a pan to cook with the remaining wine. When the wine has reduced by half, add 1.2 litres of the cooking stock. Bring it back to the boil and then pour the liquid over the meat. Fold in the mustard, carrots and parsley, and season well. Pour everything into a terrine or glass bowl, cover with clingfilm and refrigerate at least overnight. To serve, either turn out and slice or scoop out with a spoon.

WINES

With this kind of food you need wine you can quaff with abandon. Serve both the reds lightly chilled. The Pinot Blanc from the hills bordering Slovenia is also a good match for these flavours

BEAUJOLAIS MORGON
DOLE SWISS BLEND PINOT NOIR
COLLIO PINOT BLANC

Wild Boar Pâté flavoured with Juniper Berries

Remove the rind from the smoked belly pork and cut into pieces, about 1 x 3cm. Cut the wild boar leg meat the same way and add to the smoked belly. Douse with brandy, season with a little of the salt and pepper, cover and refrigerate. Put the shallots and garlic in a pan with the red wine and bring to the boil. Add thyme and bay leaf, and reduce until almost dry. Remove the herbs and discard, leaving the shallots, garlic and wine mix to cool.

Take the rest of the meat (wild boar shoulder and belly and the pork fat) and cut up into big cubes. Season with the remaining salt and pepper and the juniper berries. Cover and refrigerate overnight. Next day, mince the meat finely, then beat well with a spatula. Add the shallots and wine mixture and finally the cubed meat (the brandy-soaked smoked belly pork and boar leg meat) with its juices.

Preheat the oven to 200°C/gas 6. Line a buttered terrine, about 20 x 30cm, with the slices of Parma ham. Let the slices hang over the sides so that they can then be used to cover the pâté. Press in the mixture and fold the slices of ham over the top. Place the terrine in a bain-marie, or a pan of water and bring to a simmer. Place in the hot oven for 15 minutes, then turn the oven down to 170°C/gas 3, cover the pâté with buttered foil and continue to cook for 40 minutes.

Leave to cool for 30 minutes. Place something flat over the terrine and add a weight of about 500g for two hours. Refrigerate overnight. Best eaten after two or three days with country-style toasted bread.

WINES

If you're using farmed boar, the Crozes-Hermitage is just the ticket. With truly wild and gamey boar, try a refreshing Chianti Classico. A Saumur-Champigny Cabernet Franc with its aromatic leafy tones will have no trouble with the density of the pâté or the fragrant juniper.

CROZES-HERMITAGE YOUNG WHITE
CHIANTI CLASSICO
SAUMUR-CHAMPIGNY CABERNET FRANC

SERVES 8–10

200g smoked belly pork
200g wild boar meat from the leg
1 tbsp brandy
1 tsp freshly ground black pepper
20g salt
2 shallots, peeled and finely chopped
1 garlic clove, peeled and finely chopped
200ml strong red wine
2 sprigs of thyme
1 bay leaf
600g wild boar meat taken from shoulder
200g wild boar meat taken from belly
300g pork fat
6 juniper berries, crushed
10–12 thin slices Parma ham

Rabbit Rillettes

SERVES 15–20

1.2kg back fat pork
bouquet garni made from
    celery stick, small piece of
    leek, 2 bay leaves, 5–6
    parsley stalks and thyme,
    all tied together with
    string
1 onion, peeled and
    studded with 2 cloves
1 carrot, peeled
3 garlic cloves, peeled
150g smoked bacon, diced
½ bottle dry white wine
salt, pepper, nutmeg
1.2 kg whole rabbit (not
    wild), boned and cut up
400g pork shoulder, cut
    into large dice
200ml dry white wine

Cut the back fat pork into small cubes, put into a large saucepan and cover with plenty of water – about 2 litres. Simmer for about an hour, until the fat has softened and become translucent and the water has evaporated. Add the bouquet garni, onion, carrot, garlic, smoked bacon and the half bottle of wine. Season generously – when cold the rillettes will taste bland if not slightly over seasoned now.

Add the rabbit and diced pork to the simmering mixture in the saucepan and stir well. Cover with parchment paper and turn down the heat so the pan barely simmers. Cook for about 2 hours, stirring occasionally, until the meat is so soft it crumbles.

Take off the heat and pour into a clean bowl set on ice. Add the 200ml of white wine and stir vigorously with a spatula until cold. The rillettes will change colour and turn opaque-white from the emulsified fat. Put the rillettes into jars or a terrine and store in the refrigerator. They keep for two or three weeks. Serve with hot toast and corni-chons.

WINES

The Gamay grape is perfect for convivial, cheerful drinking. Dolcetto d'Alba should be drunk young and works well with meat starters.

SAVOIE GAMAY
DOLCETTO D'ALBA

Chicken Liver Parfait

Once upon a time this was on every menu in the country. It's now out of fashion but due for a comeback. The foie gras is needed to give it richness.

Pour the port, Madeira and brandy into a pan and reduce until syrupy. Trim the chicken livers, making sure there are no green bile areas, which can be bitter. Put the liver and foie gras into a blender or food processor and blitz until smooth. Sweat the shallots in a little butter and allow them to cool. Melt the rest of the butter. Add the shallots, with the reduced alcohol and melted (not hot) butter in a stream to the liver mixture.

Add the eggs one by one, thyme and garlic, and continue to blitz. Season well, then pass the mixture though a fine sieve into a buttered terrine, measuring 22 x 8cm. Place in a bain-marie or a roasting pan filled with water. Bring the water in the bain-marie to a gentle simmer, cover and place in a moderate oven 150°C/gas 2 for 1½–2 hours or until set. Leave to cool and then refrigerate overnight.

To serve, remove the skin that will have formed and spoon out into quenelles with a tablespoon dipped in hot water (see opposite). Alternatively, turn the parfait out of the terrine by running a hot knife around the edges and dipping the dish into hot water for a few seconds. Then slice. Serve with melba toast, salad and chutney.

WINES

Liver is nearly always served with something sweet to eat and this also applies to drinks. Old sweetened Oloroso sherry, or even a sweet Condrieu from the hills of the Rhône valley – Viognier, the single grape variety wine – are both silky like the parfait. If you can find the spectacular Rodenbach beer from Belgium, it's well worth trying.

SWEET OLD OLOROSO SHERRY
CONDRIEU (VIOGNIER)
BELGIAN RODENBACH BEER

SERVES 10–12

100ml port
100ml Madeira
50ml brandy
200g chicken livers (cleaned weight)
200g raw foie gras
3 shallots, peeled and chopped
400g butter
5 eggs
1 sprig of thyme
1 garlic clove, peeled and sliced
salt, pepper, nutmeg

Duck Foie Gras with Confit Turnips

This is a dish that, like the foie gras terrine opposite, I first came across when I was working as a young apprentice at the great Alain Chapel restaurant in France.

SERVES 6

6 firm, medium-size
  turnips, peeled
1 tbsp caster sugar
2 tbsp duck or goose fat
salt and pepper
125ml Madeira
250ml white chicken stock
  (see page 32)
1 tbsp sherry vinegar
1 lobe duck foie gras, about
  500g

Cut the turnips into 5mm slices. Toss the slices in caster sugar and put in a wide pan with the duck fat. Cook the turnips gently, turning frequently, until they are golden all over. Season and add the Madeira. Boil until the water has almost completely evaporated, then add the stock and reduce until syrupy. The turnips should be tender but still holding together. Finally splash in the sherry vinegar.

Cut the duck foie gras into six slices and season with salt and pepper. Place in a scalding hot pan and sear well until caramelised on both sides and cooked. Check the liver is cooked by pressing with a finger – it should give slightly under the pressure. Serve with the confit turnips.

WINES

The obvious choice is the sweet white Coteaux du Layon from the Loire Valley, but the sweet red from Banyuls also works well. The velvety Pinot Noir is a good match for the meatiness of the sauce, turnips and liver.

YOUNG COTEAUX DU LAYON
BANYULS
VOSNE ROMANÉE

Fois Gras Terrine

At Alain Chapel we made this terrine with goose liver, which has a different taste and texture to duck and is more expensive — worth it, in this case, I think. Duck livers work well, but they must be the best and very fresh.

Immerse the foie gras in the milk, then cover with very cold water, season well with salt and refrigerate. Leave the liver in this bath for 3–4 hours, turning occasionally. Drain carefully and pat dry with a clean cloth. Season well with salt, pepper and a little nutmeg and place in a roasting pan, large enough for the foie gras to lie flat.

Place in a pre-heated oven at 220°/gas 7 and immediately turn the temperature down to 150°C/gas 2. After 5 minutes some of the fat of the foie gras should be starting to melt. Baste the foie gras with the fat every 5 minutes for 25 minutes, by which time the small lobes should be cooked. To check, gently squeeze the liver between thumb and forefinger – it should be very supple. Then insert a small knife or needle into the centre of a small lobes. Remove after 10 seconds and place on your lips – it should be warm. Place the small lobes in a porcelain terrine, about 20 x 8cm. Continue cooking the larger lobes for another 10 minutes, basting as before. Once they are cooked, add them to the terrine. Place another terrine or dish on top of the liver to press it down – a weight of about 500g should be enough. Refrigerate overnight. Strain the fat left in the pan and refrigerate.

Next day, take off the weight and tip out any blood and juices in the terrine – these can be used in a soup or stock. Melt the strained fat and pour over the foie gras. Cover the terrine and refrigerate until needed. It keeps for 10 days. Traditionally this terrine is not sliced but spooned. Dip a serving spoon in hot water and spoon out in generous curls. Serve with country-style bread, thinly sliced and lightly toasted.

WINES
I tend to shy away from very sweet wines with foie gras and prefer a late harvest, with a good level of acidity to balance the liver's fattiness.

PINOT GRIS VENDANGE TARDIVE
AUSTRALIAN LATE HARVEST RIESLING

SERVES 8–10
2 duck foie gras, 400g each, lobes separated into 2 at the natural separation and any green parts and large nerves and veins removed
250ml milk
salt, pepper, nutmeg

Hot Foie Gras with Honey-glazed Spiced Parsnips and Rhubarb

Rhubarb doesn't just belong in a crumble. In fact, its sharpness can be used to liven up many dishes.

SERVES 6

4 sticks rhubarb

1 vanilla pod, split

3 tbsp caster sugar

125ml veal stock
  (see page 53)

2 tbsp butter

salt and pepper

3 parsnips

vegetable oil for frying

½ tsp each of coriander
  seeds, cumin seeds and
  dry pink peppercorns,
  cracked

1 tbsp clear honey

6 slices duck foie gras,
  about 80g each

Wash and top and tail the rhubarb, then cut into 5cm batons. Put into a pan with the vanilla pod and sugar, and cover with water. Bring to the boil and immediately take off the heat. Leave to cool and then drain, reserving the syrup. Reduce the syrup with 125ml of veal stock until it has the consistency of a sauce, then whisk in 1 tablespoon of the butter bit by bit to thicken and shine. Season with salt and pepper.

Peel the parsnips and cut two into the same size batons as the rhubarb. You should get 12 batons. Blanch these in boiling salted water for 2 minutes, then refresh in iced water and drain. Slice the remaining parsnip into long wafer-thin slices. Heat some vegetable oil in a deep fryer or large pan and deep fry the parsnip slices until crisp. Drain on kitchen towel and sprinkle with salt.

Pan fry the parsnip batons with a little oil and a tablespoon of butter over a gentle heat until golden. Drain off the fat and add the spices, salt and honey. Toss the parsnips over a medium heat to glaze, then add the rhubarb to re-heat. Season the foie gras and fry in a dry pan over high heat. Gently turn when golden and lower the heat. The foie gras should take 7–8 minutes to cook, depending on its thickness. When done, it should give a little when pressed.

To serve, arrange the batons of rhubarb and parsnip on the plates. Add the foie gras, followed by the parsnip crisps. Drizzle the sauce around each serving.

WINES

An old rosé or a demi-sec Champagne both marry well with the acidity of rhubarb and the spicing. The Vouvray has enough body to cope with these flavours as does a late harvest Pinot Gris from Alsace.

CHAMPAGNE ROSÉ OR DEMI-SEC (RICH RESERVE)

VOUVRAY MOELLEUX

ALSACE PINOT GRIS VENDANGE TARDIVE

Fine Wines
Usually you choose a wine to go with the food you are serving, but sometimes, when you have a special bottle, you will want to plan the menu around it. Here are some suggestions for very fine wines and dishes to complement them.

SOAVE CLASSICO CAPITEL FOSCARINO 1999 ANSELMI

One of the few Soave from single vineyards. This wine is smooth, yet racy, rather like Roberto Anselmi himself!

Scallops à la Nage with Velvet Butter Sauce

SERVES 4
8 large scallops in the shell
1 medium carrot, peeled
4 large pickling onions
2 sticks of celery
300ml dry white wine
1 bay leaf
80ml double cream
100g butter, diced
salt and pepper
lemon juice

Always buy your scallops in the shell so you can be sure they are fresh. Remove the white meat and coral, rinse under cold water and dry gently. Remove the black stomach and discard. Take the skirt from the scallops and soak for 20 minutes in cold water, then drain.

Slice the carrot into thin rounds. If you want to make the rounds more decorative, score the carrot with a channelling knife first. Peel the onions and cut into thin rings. Peel and wash the celery sticks, and cut into 3cm batons. Put the wine in a pan with 300ml water, add salt and bring to the boil. Add the vegetables and bay leaf. Remove with a slotted spoon when cooked. Add the skirt to the liquid and simmer for 15 minutes, then press the liquid through a fine sieve. Pour half the liquid into the pan and add the cream. Bring it back to the boil and whisk in the butter a little at a time. Check the seasoning and add a little squeeze of lemon.

Lay the scallops in a pan on top of the stove and pour on the other half of the liquid. Bring to a gentle simmer and cover with greaseproof paper. After 1 minute, turn the scallops and cook for a further 2 minutes (depending on size). To assemble, drain the scallops and put on plates. Arrange the warm vegetables round them and pour on the hot sauce.

ROBERT MONDAVI WINERY
NAPA VALLEY
CHARDONNAY

CHARDONNAY NAPA 2000
ROBERT MONDAVI

The name Mondavi is synonymous with both the Napa Valley and excellence. This wine is as fat and juicy as the diver-caught Scottish scallops used in this dish, hence the pairing.

Grilled Scallops
with Crab and Herb Velouté

SERVES 8
8 scallops, 70g each
salt and pepper
olive oil
100g carrot
100g leek
30ml Chartreuse Verte
200g white crab meat

Sauce
5 shallots, peeled
7 or 8 button mushrooms
1 tbsp butter
1 glass of Champagne
200ml fish stock
200ml double cream
1 tbsp each of chives,
    chervil, flat-leaf parsley,
    chopped
1 tbsp Chartreuse Verte
salt

Fish stock
1kg fish bones and heads
1 small onion, chopped
1 stick of celery, chopped
60g butter
100ml dry white wine
6 parsley stalks
1 bay leaf

Take the scallops out of their shells and trim and clean (see page 68). Season them with salt, pepper and olive oil and cook on a grilling pan for 3–4 minutes. Cut the carrot and leek into julienne strips and sweat in olive oil until cooked but still crunchy, then deglaze with the Chartreuse. Add the crab meat and season. Serve in deep plates or wide bowls. Arrange a bed of vegetables and crab meat on each plate, place a scallop on top and pour the sauce around.

Sauce Slice the shallots and mushrooms and sweat in butter, but don't allow them to colour. Deglaze with the Champagne and reduce by two-thirds. Add the fish stock and reduce by half. Add the cream and cook for another 20 minutes. Pass through a fine sieve. Before serving blitz in food processor with the herbs and Chartreuse to a foamy, light consistency. Season.

Fish stock Remove any gills from the fish heads. Soak the heads and bones in cold water for 3–4 hours. Roughly chop the fish bones and heads. Sweat the onion and celery with the butter in a deep saucepan over low heat. When softened, add the fish bones and heads and cook for 2–3 minutes, stirring frequently. Pour in the wine, turn up the heat and reduce by half. Add 2 litres of water and the herbs and bring to the boil, skimming frequently. Lower the heat and simmer, uncovered, for 25 minutes. Strain the stock through a sieve lined with muslin and leave to cool. This makes about 2 litres – more than you need for this recipe but the rest can be frozen.

BÂTARD-MONTRACHET GRAND CRU DOMAINE LEFLAIVE

Domaine Leflaive is one of the best white-wine makers in the Montrachet region and this is the best-balanced Chardonnay ever made. Full-tasting, the oakiness is just as it should be. Perfect.

Ragoût de Langouste et Petites Girolles

Crayfish, or langoustes in French, are not only one of the most beautiful creatures of the sea but also one of the most delicious to eat.

Bring the white wine, orange peel, thyme, bay leaf and sea salt to the boil with 1.5 litres of water. Add the crayfish and boil for 8 minutes. Take off the heat and leave to cool. When the crayfish is cool enough to handle, crack it open to extract all the meat – not forgetting the meat in the claws. Cut into bite-size pieces and set aside. Reserve the cooking liquid.

Trim the girolles and sweat in a little of the butter until they have rendered some moisture. Add the shallots and continue to cook for 1 minute. Pour in 100ml of the cooking liquid and rapidly reduce by half. Add the cream and reduce by a third. Finally whisk in the butter a little at a time until the sauce is rich and velvety.

Check the seasoning and add a few drops of lemon juice. Add the crayfish to the sauce just to warm through, but do not boil. Sprinkle with chives and serve immediately.

SERVES 6

½ litre dry white wine
1 strip of orange peel
1 sprig of thyme
1 bay leaf
3 tbsp coarse sea salt
1 crayfish (spiny lobster), about 1kg in weight
120g small girolle mushrooms
2 shallots, peeled and finely chopped
100ml double cream
160g butter, diced
salt and pepper
lemon juice
1 small bunch of chives, snipped into small pieces

RIESLING 1997
CUVÉE DES COMTES D'EGUISHEIM
LÉON BEYER

This has a wonderfully dense, mineral flavour. It is a very masculine Riesling — versatile, strong and full of character like its owner. In fact, I've often noticed how wines resemble the people who make them.

Spicy Crab Cakes

SERVES 8

500g crab claw meat

2 shallots, peeled and chopped

1 sprig coriander

1 sprig opal basil

2 dry chillies

60g Japanese breadcrumbs (Panko), plus extra for dusting

juice of half a lemon

salt and pepper

1 tsp sugar

1 whole egg

2 tbsp Dijon mustard

4 tbsp mayonnaise

vegetable oil for frying

Ginger and Spring Onion Crème Fraîche

50g fresh ginger

125g crème fraîche

3 spring onions, sliced

salt and pepper

juice of lemon

green Tabasco to taste

Make sure the crab is clean and there are no bones or cartilage. Mix the chopped shallots, coriander, basil and chillies and add to the crab. Gently fold in the breadcrumbs, lemon juice, seasoning, sugar, egg, mustard and mayonnaise, then refrigerate the mixture for an hour.

Press into small cakes about 2cm deep and dust with the extra Panko crumbs. Pan fry in a non-stick pan with a little vegetable oil until golden both sides. Serve with wedges of lime and salad and the sauce on the side.

Ginger and Spring Onion Crème Fraîche Peel the ginger and dice very finely — a Japanese vegetable slicer helps. Fold the ginger into the crème fraîche with the sliced spring onions. Season to taste with salt, pepper, lemon juice and Tabasco.

VONDELING 2004 SAUVIGNON BLANC

This crisp Sauvignon Blanc from the Paarl region of South Africa is probably not the best example of its kind, but perfect for shellfish. Believe me, these particular winemakers are setting their sights very high – definitely a wine to watch.

Plateau de Fruits de Mer

This is the kind of platter you see in the big brasseries in Paris and in restaurants up and down the north and west coasts of France – less so on the Mediterranean shores. Most of the seafood in this platter is raw. Although it is wonderful to eat this kind of food in summer, I would avoid it and follow the old rule of eating seafood only when there's an 'r' in the month. Vary the seafood according to what you can find and your personal taste.

To cook the whelks, boil in heavily salted water for 20–30 minutes depending on size. Boil the winkles in the same way but only for 3–4 minutes. These can be bought ready cooked along with the langoustines and crab. Keep the langoustines whole and cut the crabs in half with a big knife or a cleaver. Leave the oysters, sea urchins and clams raw and open with an oyster knife just before eating. Serve on crushed ice and seaweed, with some wedges of lemon, Tabasco, mayonnaise and the shallot vinegar.

Mayonnaise Whisk the egg yolks, lemon juice, mustard, salt, pepper together and slowly pour in the oil.

Shallot vinegar Peel and finely chop the shallots, add to the vinegar and leave to steep for an hour before serving.

SERVES 4

12 whelks
320g winkles
8 langoustines cooked
2 small cock crabs cooked
12 native oysters
12 rock oysters
4 sea urchins
8 palourdes clams
20 amandes clams

Mayonnaise
2 egg yolks
1 tbsp lemon juice
1 tbsp Dijon mustard
salt and pepper
200ml vegetable oil or
  groundnut oil
50ml extra virgin olive oil

Shallot vinegar
4 shallots
100ml red wine vinegar

The Main Course

Pairing food and wine should not be daunting. Foods have different flavours, textures and aromas and so do wines. The trick is to find the ones that not only work together, but also enhance each other.

Think of acidity in wine like lemon juice on an oyster or a piece of fish. Dishes that need a squeeze of lemon usually go well with fresh, zesty wines that have a little sharpness to them.

Full wines, red or white, have an almost mouth-filling texture. These would overwhelm delicate food and need dishes that are equally robust, rich in flavour and texture.

You also need to consider the sauce – rich meat-based, light and acidic, creamy, tomato-based and so on. A plain poached piece of turbot, for example, will need a different wine to a piece of the same fish roasted with a port jus.

Finally, look at the cooking method as this may also affect your choice. Poaching usually indicates lighter dishes, roasting entails caramelisation, grilling gives a slight carbon bitter taste to the food, a gratin usually involves cheese .

Romanée-Conti 1971, Domaine de la Romanée-Conti
This is one of several appellations from this Burgundy area. It is the only domaine that produces solely grand cru wines. It goes especially well with white meat, such as veal and chicken, but also with any meat or game.

Monkfish Stew with Garlic

Known as bourride in French, this monkfish stew is a joy to cook and to eat. Mopping up the broth with big chunks of bread at the end tastes almost too good to be true.

SERVES 6
1.5kg monkfish
2 onions, peeled and thinly
    sliced
2 fennel, peeled and thinly
    sliced
2 carrots, peeled and thinly
    sliced
1 leek
2 tbsp olive oil
2 bay leaves
salt and pepper
250ml dry white wine
250ml aïoli

Aïoli
10 garlic cloves
2 yolks
juice of 1 lemon
salt and pepper
250ml olive oil
1 tsp Dijon mustard

Clean the monkfish, remove the outer membrane and cut into six equal pieces. Leave the pieces on the bone. Prepare the onion, fennel and carrots. Slice and wash the leek, using only the white part. Sweat the vegetables in a large pan with a little olive oil until tender. Add the bay leaves and a little seasoning. Pour over the wine and 250ml of water and simmer for 10 minutes.

Season the monkfish and pan fry in a non-stick pan over high heat for only 3–4 minutes in total. Remove the fish from the frying pan and add to the vegetables. Cover with a loose-fitting lid and simmer gently for 8–10 minutes. When the monkfish is cooked, take in out with a slotted spoon and whisk the aïoli into the vegetable broth. The vegetables should break up and the broth should take on the consistency of a thick soup. Do not re-boil once the aïoli has been incorporated or it may separate. Serve immediately in deep bowls.

Aïoli Peel the garlic and remove the central green germ from any of the cloves. Place in a mortar or a blender and process, gradually adding all the other ingredients, until you have a smooth paste.

WINES
This is a classic Mediterranean dish that cries out for local wine. The Rosé de Provence made from Grenache, Cinsault and a hint of Syrah, has a fragrant, yet cleansing palate. Cassis white has its own particular leafy taste and is a wine that the locals drink with fish stews. Rias Baixas in northern Spain produces some stunning whites that go with fish and seafood – very different and worth a try.

ROSÉ DE PROVENCE
CASSIS WHITE
GALICIAN WHITE

Red Mullet with Ceps and Red Wine Sauce

SERVES 6

600g veal marrow bones

3 red mullet, about 400g
  each

6 shallots, peeled

1 stick of celery, chopped

2 tbsp caster sugar

1 tbsp red wine vinegar

125ml strong dark red wine

260ml veal stock

2 tbsp butter

20g extra bitter dark
  chocolate

6 slices of baguette bread

1 garlic clove, cut in half

400g cep mushrooms
  (cèpes)

1 bunch of flat-leaf parsley,
  chopped

olive oil

salt and pepper

Crack the veal marrow bones open to reveal the marrow. This can be dangerous and if you're not used to using a cleaver, ask your butcher to do this for you. Keep the marrow in large cylinder-like pieces and put in iced salted water to disgorge until needed. Scale, fillet and pin bone the fish, rinse and dry on a paper towel. Season the fillets, brush with oil and place on a baking sheet ready to be cooked.

In a saucepan with a little oil, sweat 3 sliced shallots and the chopped celery until lightly coloured. Add the rinsed fish bones and continue to cook for 3–4 minutes. Add the sugar, vinegar and red wine, then simmer until reduced by half. Add the stock and simmer, skimming well, for 20 minutes. Pass the liquid through a very fine sieve. Just before serving, check seasoning, bring back to the boil and whisk in the butter and chocolate a little at a time.

Pan fry the slices of baguette in olive oil until brown and crisp. Remove from the pan and when cool enough to handle, rub with the garlic. Trim, clean and slice the ceps. Pan fry them over high heat with a little oil until almost cooked, then finely chop the remaining shallots and add them to the pan. Continue to cook for 2–3 minutes and add the parsley.

Slice the marrow into 1cm rounds, place in simmering salted water and poach for 5 minutes until tender. Gently drain and divide equally between the baguette slices.

Cook the red mullet under a hot grill – the skin should bubble and brown slightly. Place the fish on top of the ceps and the baguette slices on top of the fish.

WINES

The meaty red mullet and red wine sauce need a wine with structure, but not so powerful that it overwhelms the fish. Otago produces some of the best Pinot Noir around, delicate yet assertive. Bourgeuil, a Cabernet Franc, is definitely brawny enough, as is a young red Bandol.

OTAGO NEW ZEALAND PINOT NOIR

BOURGEUIL

YOUNG BANDOL RED

Red Mullet with Jerusalem Artichokes, Fennel and Lobster Jus

This red mullet recipe is equally robust but can be accompanied by white wine.

Cook the artichokes in salted water. When they are done, cut 8 chunky wedges and fry in a tablespoon of olive oil and a knob of butter until nice and golden. Blitz the remaining artichokes in a blender and pass through a fine sieve if necessary. Hang in a muslin cloth to drain off the excess water. When ready to serve, boil the cream, add the artichoke purée and the butter, a little at a time. Check seasoning.

Peel and roast the whole fennel bulb in a tablespoon of olive oil for 5–6 minutes. When golden all over, add the fennel seeds, deglaze with the wine and reduce by half. Add the chicken stock, bouquet garni and seasoning. Cover with greaseproof paper and braise in the oven, at 180°C/gas 4, for 30 minutes. When the fennel is cooked, slice into 8 wedges and colour both sides in olive oil before serving.

Clean the fish and take the fillets off the bone. Season with salt, pepper and olive oil, and cook under a hot grill, skin side up. Serve the fish on a bed of artichoke purée, artichokes and fennel with the sauce.

Lobster jus Sweat the crushed lobster heads with the vegetable mirepoix in olive oil until they are golden. Add the tomato purée and fresh tomatoes. Deglaze with the cognac and wine, then flambé. Reduce by two-thirds and add the stocks and herbs. Cook for about 1 hour and pass through a fine conical sieve. Reduce to a jus consistency and add the butter, a little at a time, to thicken and shine the sauce before serving.

WINES
The sweetness of the lobster jus and the artichokes demands a different style of wine for the same fish. The Condrieu is slightly sweet and fruity. The Saint Joseph, from the north of the Rhône Valley is equally packed with fruit but red. A very different choice would be a Seyval blend from Kent.

CONDRIEU SAINT JOSEPH RED
ENGLISH SEYVAL BLEND

SERVES 8
500g Jerusalem artichokes, peeled
olive oil
50g butter, diced plus extra for frying the artichokes
100g double cream
1 large fennel bulb
1 tbsp fennel seeds
200ml white wine
250ml chicken stock (see page 32)
1 bouquet garni
salt and pepper
4 red mullet, 450g each

Lobster jus
500g lobster heads
mirepoix of vegetables made with 1 onion, 2 shallots, 1 carrot, trimmings from fennel bulb and 1 celery stick, all peeled or trimmed and diced
1 tbsp olive oil
1 tbsp tomato purée
100g fresh tomatoes
splash of cognac
200ml white wine
1 litre fish stock (see page 70)
300ml veal stock (see page 53)
herb stalks: basil, tarragon, parsley, chervil
2 tbsp butter, diced

Red Mullet with an Orange Almond Crust

Mediterranean flavours this time for this most versatile of fish.

SERVES 6

3 red mullet, about 400g
  each
120g butter, softened
2 tbsp white dry
  breadcrumbs
2 tbsp ground almonds
2 tsp thyme leaves,
  chopped
1 tbsp parsley, chopped
1 tbsp coarsely cracked
  black/white pepper
grated zest and juice of 1
  orange
3 tomatoes
3 courgettes
olive oil
salt and pepper
juice of 1 lemon
1 small bunch of basil

Scale, fillet and remove the pin bones from the fish. Rinse and dry with paper towel. Place the fillets on a lightly oiled and seasoned baking tray.

Whisk the softened butter and add the breadcrumbs, ground almonds, thyme, parsley, pepper and finally the orange juice and zest. Place in the fridge for 10 minutes to set.

Blanch the tomatoes in boiling water, refresh and remove the skins. Cut in half, de-seed, roughly chop and set aside. Slice the courgettes and put them in a pan with a little olive oil. Season well and cook until lightly coloured but still crunchy. Add the tomatoes so they just warm through. Add the lemon juice and a little more olive oil and toss in the basil leaves.

Preheat the oven to 200°C/gas 6. Make the almond paste into shapes the same size as your mullet fillets and place one on top of each piece of fish. Bake in the hot oven for 4 minutes and then put under the grill to finish off cooking and to give the crust a golden brown colour. Divide the tomato and courgette mixture between the plates and serve the fish on top.

WINES

Mullet again, but different wines. All three of these wines are fragrant with good levels of acidity, but that's where the similarity ends. All three work in harmony with the flavours in this recipe.

SANCERRE RED
BELLET ROSÉ
PALETTE BLANC

Poached Pike in Butter Sauce

*Pike used to be a popular table fish, along with carp, perch and barbel.
Make sure you choose a pike from clear running water or else it may be
a little muddy in taste.*

Peel the carrots, run a channelling knife round them to give a star
shape, then slice. Peel the onions and slice into rings. Make a bouquet
garni by tying the celery, thyme, bay, parsley together.

To make the court bouillon, put the wine in a pan with 125ml of
water. Bring to the boil and add the carrots, onions, bouquet garni, salt
and peppercorns. Simmer for 5 minutes, then cover and leave to cool.
Remove the vegetables and set aside.

Clean the pike by removing the gills, guts and eyes. Rinse well and
dry. Place in a fish kettle and cover with the cold court bouillon. Cover
and bring to a very gentle simmer for 16 minutes, then turn off the
heat. Serve the fish whole with the vegetables from the court bouillon
and the butter sauce.

Butter sauce Take 200ml of the poaching liquid and reduce by half
over a high heat. Add the double cream and reduce by half again.
Whisk in the cold butter a little at a time. Check the seasoning and add
a squeeze of lemon juice.

WINES

This dish needs a velvety rounded wine and all three listed have this
quality. No chance to paper over the cracks here, so quality is vital.

VOUVRAY
ALSACE RIESLING GRAND CRU
CHABLIS GRAND CRU

SERVES 6
2 carrots
4 onions small
1 stick of celery
1 sprig of thyme
2 bay leaves
1 sprig parsley
750ml dry white wine
1 tbsp sea salt
1 tbsp white peppercorns
1 pike, about 2kg in weight

Butter sauce
100ml double cream
200g cold butter, diced
salt and pepper
lemon juice

Braised Trout in Riesling

This is a really simple recipe that lets the food and wine do the talking.
The straightforward matching of food and wine need not be complex.

SERVES 4

4 trout, 200–240g each

60g butter

2 shallots, peeled and finely
  chopped

6 button mushrooms,
  washed and sliced

250ml Riesling wine

salt and pepper

200ml double cream

lemon juice

Prepare the trout by snipping off the fins and removing the gills and eyes. Rinse well under cold water and pat dry with kitchen paper.

Preheat the oven to 200°C/gas 6. Take a shallow ovenproof dish that can be used on the top of the stove and smear with a little butter. Sprinkle the shallots and mushrooms into the dish and lay the trout on top. Pour in the wine and season. Cover with a buttered foil, bring to a simmer and place in the oven for 8–10 minutes.

Remove the trout and pass the cooking liquid through a fine sieve into a pan. Bring to the boil and reduce by half. Add the cream and reduce again until sauce consistency. Finish by whisking in the remaining butter, cut into small dice, check the seasoning and add a squeeze of lemon juice.

To serve, remove the skin from the trout and spoon over the sauce. Accompany with boiled potatoes and peas.

WINES

Riesling is the obvious drink when you're cooking with the stuff! Make it a young dry wine from Alsace. If you want something else, a 'flinty' Sauvignon, such as a Reuilly or Pouilly Fumé, won't break the bank but will give you ample satisfaction.

RIESLING (YOUNG AND DRY)

REUILLY

POUILLY FUMÉ

Grilled Sardines with Ham and Basil, and Tomato Relish

Sardines are meaty morsels that need acidity to combat their oiliness — hence the tomato relish and lemony-fresh wines. To make this a real classic, serve on toast.

SERVES 6

18 sardines

1 bunch of basil

pepper

9 thin slices of Parma ham

Tomato relish

8 large plum tomatoes

3 shallots, peeled and chopped

4 garlic cloves, peeled and chopped

2 tbsp malt vinegar

1 tbsp tomato paste

2 tbsp muscovado sugar

salt and pepper

pinch of chilli powder

1 tbsp each of mint, basil and coriander, roughly chopped

Clean the sardines — scrape off the scales, cut off the heads and remove the guts. Take out the backbone by running a knife down the back of each fish and pulling out the bones. Leave the tail end attached. Gently rinse and dry with kitchen paper.

Place 3 or 4 basil leaves on a sardine fillet, season with pepper and place another fillet on top. Wrap each pair of fillets in a slice of ham and hold together with a wooden cocktail stick. Grill for 4 minutes each side and serve with the relish. If you want to serve the sardines with toast, grill some slices of sourdough bread and rub with a little garlic. Top with some relish followed by the sardines.

Tomato relish Blanch the tomatoes and skin. De-seed them and chop roughly. Put the shallots and garlic in a pan with the vinegar and 2 tablespoons of water. Simmer until almost dry, then add the tomato paste and sugar. Continue to cook and stir for 3–4 minutes. Add the tomato flesh, season to taste with salt, pepper and chilli powder and simmer for 10–12 minutes until cooked. When cool, fold in the roughly chopped herbs.

WINES

A young, slightly fizzy Vinho Verde from Portugal is always nice with sardines, but try a Gavi from the Piedmont region of Italy and you'll be pleasantly surprised. Muscadet is always a good choice.

VINHO VERDE

GAVI DI GAVI

MUSCADET

Salt Cod 'Rougail'

French Creole in style, rougail is a traditional dish in Mauritius. For this recipe it's vital to have a thick piece of cod, the thicker the better.

Soak the cod, skin-side up, in plenty of cold water for 36 hours, changing the water frequently. Afterwards, rinse the fish and place it in a large pan. Cover with cold water and bring to a gentle simmer for 4–5 minutes. Take off the heat and leave to cool. Gently take the fish out and dry on a clean cloth. Remove any bones and cut into 6 equal portions, discarding any thin or belly parts.

In a non-stick pan with a smear of oil, fry the fish flesh-side down until golden. Remove and set aside in a warm place. In the same pan add the remaining oil and sweat the onions over medium heat stirring with a spatula until soft. Add the garlic and continue to cook for another 5 minutes. Blanch the tomatoes to remove the skin, de-seed and roughly chop. Add the tomatoes to the pan, with the thyme, turmeric and chillies, turn up the heat and simmer for 5 minutes.

Preheat the oven to 180°C/gas 4. Turn the tomato mixture into an ovenproof serving dish and place the fish on top with any juices that have run. Loosely cover with a piece of oiled foil and bake in the oven for 8–10 minutes. Serve with lime wedges and decorate with coriander.

WINES
Sherry always works with the salt and spice of this dish. A top-quality Sauvignon from New Zealand will have enough bite, as does a typical Austrian wine made from the popular Grüner Veitliner grape.

DRY MANZANILLA SHERRY
NEW ZEALAND SAUVIGNON BLANC
GRÜNER VEITLINER

SERVES 6

1.2kg salt cod
100ml vegetable oil
2 onions, peeled and finely chopped
4 garlic cloves, peeled and finely chopped
10 plum tomatoes
1 sprig of thyme
1 tbsp turmeric
2 large mild chillies, 1 red and 1 green, thinly sliced
2–4 piment oiseaux, tiny very hot chillies
2 limes
1 bunch of fresh coriander, chopped

Normandy-style Roast Mackerel

This is another meaty and oily fish. Make sure it's glistening when you buy it — a sure sign of freshness. I cooked this dish on the rocks in Ireland after fishing for mackerel. The fish was so fresh it was almost jumping into my camping gas frying pan!

SERVES 4

4 mackerel, about 300g
  each
2 tbsp Dijon mustard
2 tbsp vegetable oil
salt and pepper
4 apples, Russet or Cox
2 shallots, peeled and sliced
6 white button
  mushrooms, washed
  and sliced
1 tbsp butter
250ml dry cider
125ml crème fraîche

Clean the mackerel: remove the heads and fins and once gutted, wash and pat dry with kitchen paper. Slash across the flesh on both sides 4 times and brush each fish with the mustard.

Preheat the oven to 220°C/gas 7. On top of the stove, heat a non-stick fish pan or roasting tray big enough for the fish. Add the oil and when it's smoking hot, gently place the fish in the pan. Lightly season and cook for a couple of minutes. Turn when nicely browned and cook for a couple of minutes more. Place in the hot oven for a further 6 minutes.

Cut the apples into wedges, then 'turn' or give them a spherical shape. Keep the trimmings. When the fish is cooked, remove from the pan and set aside in a warm place. Return the pan to the top of the stove and sweat the shallots, apple trimmings and mushrooms with a knob of fresh butter for 2–3 minutes. Stir well, pour on the cider and reduce by half. Add the crème fraîche and again reduce by half. Check the seasoning, then press the sauce through a fine sieve.

Pan fry the apple wedges in the remaining butter until golden and cooked. Serve with the mackerel and a drizzle of the sauce.

WINES

Normandy style means apples, cream and cider. For this dish, the cider should be dry and bottle-conditioned. As for wines, look for body and acidity because of the fattiness of the fish. Sauvignon Blanc springs to mind as well as Verduzzo, a little-known muscular white from the northeast of Italy.

DRY CIDER, BOTTLE-CONDITIONED
TOURAINE SAUVIGNON BLANC
VERDUZZO

Chicken Tajine with Olives and Preserved Lemons

With its gutsy flavours, this is a traditional North African dish. Preserved lemons give a slightly bitter sharpness.

SERVES 6

1 corn-fed chicken, about
  1.8kg

olive oil

2 onions, peeled and sliced

salt and pepper

2 garlic cloves, peeled and
  chopped

2 tsp turmeric

2 tsp paprika

2 tsp coriander seeds,
  cracked

300ml white chicken stock
  (see page 32) or vegetable
  stock

260g large green olives,
  pitted

2 preserved lemons cut into
  wedges

1 bunch of fresh coriander,
  chopped

Cut up the chicken into drumsticks, wings, thighs, and breasts. Cut the thighs and breasts into two. Heat a little olive oil in a frying pan and cook the sliced onions over a high heat until soft and caramelised. Put them into a tajine dish or an ovenproof pot.

Preheat the oven to 170°C/gas 3. Season the chicken pieces, add a little more oil to the frying pan and fry the chicken until golden. Turn down the heat and add the chopped garlic, turmeric, paprika and cracked coriander seeds. Cook for a few minutes to bring out the flavours, then add the stock, bring to the boil and pour into the tajine dish. Sprinkle over the olives and preserved lemons. Cover and put in the preheated oven for 45 minutes. Remove the lid, check the seasoning and drizzle in a little olive oil. Garnish with fresh coriander leaves. Serve with bulgur wheat.

WINES

These punchy flavours demand an equally raunchy wine. This Gris wine is a white made from red grapes – the best is from Morocco. Rioja is a sun-drenched wine and so has an affinity with olives, and so, strangely enough, does the Touraine.

NORTH AFRICAN 'GRIS'

RIOJA

CABERNET DE TOURAINE

Rabbit Paella

Who says paella has to be made with bits of chicken and seafood? In inland Spain, rabbit and ham are the traditional ingredients for paella and in my view they are far better.

Bone the rabbit, or ask your butcher to do this for you, and cut it into bite-size pieces. Remove the rinds from the bacon and set aside. Put the rabbit bones in a large pot, cover with water and add the bacon rinds. Bring to the boil and simmer for 25 minutes. Strain the stock and keep for later – you should have about 800ml.

Grill the peppers until their skins have turned black. Cover with clingfilm and leave to cool. When the peppers are cool enough to handle, peel off the blackened skin, remove the seeds and cores and slice into long strips.

Preheat the oven to 180°C/gas 4. In a large ovenproof pan, sweat the onions in plenty of olive oil for 2–3 minutes. Don't let them colour. Add the peppers and rice and continue to cook for 3–4 minutes, stirring well. Stir in the rabbit, tomato paste, bay leaves, saffron, chilli and seasoning, then pour on the reserved stock and quickly bring to the boil. Turn down the heat and lay the slices of bacon over the rice and rabbit. Cover with greaseproof paper and place in the oven for 25 minutes. Remove from the oven and leave in a warm place for 10 minutes to finish cooking.

WINES

Sherry may not be the obvious first choice, but it is the everyday drink in Spain. However, these meaty rustic rosés from the Basque region are perfect for washing down the local cuisine.

MANZANILLA SHERRY
DRY SPANISH ROSÉ
IROULEGUY ROSÉ

SERVES 8
1 whole rabbit (not wild)
16 slices of smoked bacon, very thinly sliced and rinds removed
3 green peppers
2 onions, peeled and chopped
olive oil
500g paella rice or long-grain rice
1 tbsp tomato paste
2 bay leaves
pinch of pure saffron
2 tsp Espelette chilli powder (this is from the Basque region of Spain)
salt and pepper

Duck Confit and Sauté Potatoes

Canard Gras is a duck that has been reared for foie gras. It will weigh about 6kg and may seem expensive, but inside is a whole foie gras.

SERVES 8

1 Canard Gras, or use
   8 large duck legs or
   2 normal ducks
1kg good-quality coarse
   sea salt
1 sprig of sage
1 sprig of thyme
1kg duck or goose fat

Sauté potatoes

1kg potatoes (Amandine,
   Belle de Fontenay or
   similar), washed and
   boiled in their skins
salt and pepper
3 garlic cloves, chopped
1 bunch of flat-leaf parsley,
   chopped

If using a Canard Gras, remove the legs and breasts, trimming off any excess fat. Chop off the head and discard. Remove the skin from the neck and add to the fat, and put the neck with the meat. Take out the foie gras, wrap in clingfilm and refrigerate to use in another recipe. Add the heart and the gizzard, cut in half and washed, to the meat.

Now trim all the skin and fat off the carcass. Keep the bones to make a stock for another recipe. Put all the fat in a pan and cover with cold water. Bring to a gentle simmer to render. This usually takes about an hour – the water should be totally evaporated and the fat clear. Pour the fat through a fine conical sieve without pressing.

Liberally sprinkle the meat with the sea salt and refrigerate for 90 minutes. Wipe off all the salt and moisture with a cloth and put the meat into the warm fat with the sage and thyme. Bring to a very gentle simmer, cover with a greaseproof paper and cook until tender, about 2 hours. The slower and longer it cooks the better. Leave to cool in the fat, then refrigerate. It will keep for several weeks.

When you want to eat the duck confit, lift the meat out of the fat and place, skin-side down, in a non-stick pan over a medium heat until crispy and golden. Turn over and put in a preheated oven (180°C/gas 4) to finish warming through for 10–15 minutes. Serve with sauté potatoes. The heart and gizzard can be eaten too.

Sauté potatoes Peel the potatoes when cool. Cut into 5mm slices and pan fry in the duck fat. Season and sprinkle with garlic and parsley.

WINES

This rustic dish needs a local wine to do it justice. A Cahors wine made from the Malbec grape is a good choice, as is the equally rustic Basque red, with a good level of tannins. Or, try a spicy Shiraz from Victoria.

CAHORS
IROULEGUY RED
AUSTRALIAN SHIRAZ

Lambs' Tongues with Watercress

Tender lambs' tongues prepared this way are divine and I defy anyone not to enjoy them. Stop being squeamish and try this recipe.

SERVES 6

12 lambs' tongues

2 sprigs of thyme

2 bay leaves

salt and pepper

2 bunches of watercress

1 carrot, peeled and
   finely diced

2 shallots, peeled and
   finely diced

1 tbsp butter

125ml dry white wine

3 tbsp crème fraîche

a pinch of cayenne pepper

1 tbsp olive oil

Rinse the tongues under cold water and place in a pot with enough cold water to cover. Add the thyme, bay leaves and salt and bring to the boil. Skim well and simmer gently for 45 minutes or until tender. Leave to cool until the water is hand hot. Take out the tongues, peel off the outer skin and slice in half lengthways. Set aside the cooking liquid. Pick over the watercress, keeping only the leaves and small buds.

Sweat the diced carrots and shallots with the butter in a wide pan for 5–6 minutes until tender – don't allow them to colour. Increase the heat and add the wine. Reduce by half and add 125ml of the tongue cooking liquid. Bring to the boil, then whisk in the crème fraîche. Season with salt, pepper and cayenne, and bring back to the boil. Keep warm. Pan fry the lambs' tongues in a non-stick pan with a drizzle of olive oil until lightly browned.

At the last second before serving, add the watercress to the warm sauce. To serve, place some sauce on each plate with slices of tongue on top.

WINES

A lightly oaked Chardonnay suits this recipe well, as does a young, fresh Dolcetto from the Piedmont, with its beautiful purple hue. A fruity Chianti from Florence will definitely tingle the tongues.

CALIFORNIAN CHARDONNAY

DOLCETTO

CHIANTI

Veal Kidneys in Three Mustard Sauce

Probably my father's all-time favourite dish...or at least one of them! And by popular demand, it's also a regular on the menu at Le Gavroche.

If the kidneys are in their fat, tear off the fat to reveal the kidney and with the point of a knife, remove all the sinews from the inside of the kidneys. Chop the fat and render it down by covering with cold water and simmering for about 2 hours until clear. Pass the fat through a very fine sieve and refrigerate until needed – it's excellent for frying chips and roasting meats.

Cut the kidneys into bite-size pieces, following the natural ridges, as closely as possible. Put a splash of oil in a large thick pan and heat until smoking hot. Add the kidneys to the pan and season. Leave for about 30 seconds without shaking or turning so the pan has time to regain heat and the kidneys take on some colour. Then cook for 3–4 minutes, turning the kidneys until nicely coloured on all sides. Take off the heat and place the kidneys in a colander to drain – they release a good deal of liquid.

Put a knob of butter in the same saucepan over a high heat and sweat the shallots. Keep stirring so they don't burn. Once the shallots are tender, pour in the brandy, followed by the wine and reduce by half. Add the cream and reduce by one-third. Take the pan off the heat and whisk in the mustards. Fold in the kidneys to re-heat gently for a couple of minutes, but do not allow them to boil – that would make the sauce bitter. Serve immediately with fresh pasta.

WINES
This dish is powerful, tangy and chewy so you need a wine of the same description. Côte Rôtie – rich and complex, made mostly with Syrah grapes – is one of the finest Rhône wines. Argentinian Malbec, sometime described as 'animal', will take no prisoners, and some of the new Cabernet blends from Chile are genuine 'grown-up' wines.

CÔTE RÔTIE
ARGENTINIAN MALBEC
SANTIAGO CHILEAN CABERNET SAUVIGNON BLEND

SERVES 6
2 veal kidneys, fat removed
olive oil
knob of butter
3 shallots, peeled and
    chopped
2 tbsp brandy
40ml dry white wine
400ml double cream
1 tbsp Dijon mustard
1 tbsp wholegrain mustard
1 tbsp tarragon or herb
    mustard
salt and pepper

Grilled Marinated Beef Cantonese, Barbecue Style

This is delicious cooked on the barbecue or simply pan fried in a non-stick pan without any fat. It can even be cooked under a hot grill. I use this recipe for little canapés served at Le Gavroche before a meal. As a main course, serve with stir-fried or grilled vegetables, or rice.

SERVES 4

500g beef sirloin (trimmed
  weight), no fat or sinew
2 tbsp tomato ketchup
1 tbsp clear honey
1 tbsp dark soy sauce
1 piece fresh ginger 4cm
  long, peeled and finely
  chopped
2 garlic cloves, peeled and
  finely chopped
½ tbsp coarsely ground
  black/white pepper
1 tbsp Worcestershire sauce
1 tbsp sesame oil

Slice the beef against the grain into thin, 3mm slices. Mix all the remaining ingredients together to make the marinade. Cover the beef with the mixture and leave to marinate for at least 2 hours but no more than 12.

Remove the meat from the marinade. Cook over high heat on a barbecue or in a non-stick pan to caramelise and serve immediately.

WINES

Try a strong, assertive Riesling that has aged for a few years. South Australian vineyards produce the richest styles from this grape. If you prefer a red, an Australian Shiraz, high in alcohol and tannin, will match this beefy spicy dish. Alternatively, warm Saké is a favourite of my father's.

OLD SOUTH AUSTRALIAN RIESLING
AUSTRALIAN SHIRAZ
WARM SAKÉ

Yorkshire and Black Pudding

Yorkshire pudding is so versatile you can use it as a base for a starter, main course or dessert. In this recipe, it's served with a good blood sausage. Look for sausage in real natural casings as the artificial ones taste, as well as look, industrial.

SERVES 8

3 eggs, beaten
250g plain flour, sifted
1 tsp salt
500–600ml milk
dripping or vegetable oil
  for cooking
1kg best quality English
  black pudding

Onion gravy
3 onions, peeled and sliced
2 tbsp butter
1 tbsp olive oil
100ml dry white wine
100ml sweet Madeira
300ml veal stock
  (see page 53)
salt and pepper
1 sprig of thyme, leaves
  picked off

Mix the eggs with the flour and salt. Using a whisk, gradually mix in the milk until you have a batter with a pouring consistency. Pass through a sieve to make sure there are no lumps and leave to rest for half an hour.

Preheat the oven to 220°C/gas 7. Heat flan dishes or pudding tins, about 6 x 8cm, and pour in a generous quantity of dripping or vegetable oil. When the oil is smoking hot, pour in the batter and place in the oven. Cook the Yorkshire puddings for 10–12 minutes until crisp on the sides.

Cut the black pudding into 1cm slices. Fry in a little vegetable oil on both sides until hot. Place the slices onto the hot puddings and serve with onion gravy.

Onion gravy Brown the onions with 1 tablespoon of butter and the olive oil over a high heat. Turn down the heat and continue to cook until soft and caramelised. Add the wine and Madeira, then boil until reduced by half. Add the stock and reduce again by a third. Whisk in the remaining butter, season and add the thyme leaves.

WINES

If the black pudding is lightly spiced, the Saint Joseph is a perfect wine. If it's heavily spiced, go for a stronger but supple Syrah from Ardèche. But perhaps the best choice of all would be a good brown ale.

SAINT JOSEPH RED
ARDÈCHE SYRAH
NEWCASTLE BROWN ALE

Grilled Neck-end Pork Chops, Oriental Style

I find neck-end chops tastier than loin chops because they have some fat running through them. These chops are particularly tasty when grilled, and perfect cooked on the barbecue.

Peel and purée the garlic, then mix with the oyster, fish and soy sauces, honey, orange juice and pepper to make the marinade. Rub this on to the chops and refrigerate for 2 hours before grilling.

WINES

The red grape of Savoie makes a deep-coloured wine that is surprisingly supple and works with white or dark meat, especially as this marinade is mild. The Pinotage is a cross between Pinot Noir and Cinsault. When good, it's very good and almost sweet. If you'd like white, the Pinot Grigio has enough roundness to drink with meat.

MONDEUSE
PINOTAGE
PINOT GRIGIO

SERVES 6
3 garlic cloves
2 tbsp oyster sauce
2 tbsp fish sauce (nam pla)
3 tbsp light soy sauce
1 tbsp honey
juice of 1 orange
plenty of coarsely ground
  pepper
6 neck-end pork chops,
  rind off, about 150g each

Pork Pie with Chestnut and Apples

This pie comes from the Cévennes, the chestnut-growing area of France. It can be eaten hot, but in my view is far better cold. You can use fresh chestnuts but they do take a long time to peel, so I recommend buying them ready cooked and peeled in vacuum packs, or dried.

SERVES 8

275g puff pastry
125g cooked ham
250g pork shoulder
200g smoked bacon
2 onions, peeled and finely
    chopped
2 tbsp olive oil
1 tbsp butter
2 garlic cloves, peeled and
    chopped
1 sprig of thyme, leaves
    picked off
2 apples, Cox or Braeburn
250g whole chestnuts
3 eggs
salt and pepper

Grease a 26cm pie or flan ring. Divide the pastry into two pieces, one slightly larger than the other. Roll out the larger piece and use to line the pie ring. Place in the refrigerator.

Mince the ham, pork and bacon. Sweat the finely chopped onions with the oil and butter until soft and translucent. Add the garlic and thyme leaves and continue to cook for 4–5 minutes. Leave to cool. Peel, core and halve the apples, then slice them finely. Fold the slices into the pork mixture with the onions, chestnuts and 2 of the eggs. Season, being generous with the pepper.

Preheat the oven to 200C/gas 6. Pack the mixture into the pie base. Beat the remaining egg. Roll out the other piece of pastry and place it on top of the pie, sealing the edges with beaten egg. Pinch the edges to make sure they are well sealed. Brush the top of the pie with egg and make a little hole in the top to let out steam. Place in the hot oven and cook for 20 minutes at 200C/gas 6, then a further 25 minutes at 180°C/gas 4. Leave to cool before removing the flan ring

WINES

Viognier de Nîmes has a refreshing sweetness and lemony fragrance and I would drink this if serving the pie warm. With cold pie, perhaps al fresco, a lightly chilled Beaujolais or a young Pinot Noir from Oregon is most enjoyable.

VIOGNIER DE NÎMES
BEAUJOLAIS VILLAGES
OREGON PINOT NOIR

Pork Shoulder Stew with Potatoes and Chorizo Sausage

This recipe for a rustic stew has its origins in the Pyrenées and it's perfect for a cold winter's night. The turnip tops are an important part of the dish, but chard can be used instead.

Be sure to ask your butcher for the bones from the pork so they can be cooked with the meat for added flavour.

Cut the pork into 3 pieces. Place in a pan with the bones and cover with cold water. Season and add the garlic and onions. Bring to a simmer, skim well and leave to cook gently for 1½ hours. The pork should be tender by the end of the cooking time. Remove the meat from the pan and slice thickly. Cover and set aside. Discard the bones.

Peel the potatoes and cut them into large chunks. Add them to the pan you used for the pork and cook for 25 minutes or until tender. You may need to top up the pan with boiling water occasionally.

Once the potatoes are cooked, add the chorizo, cut into halves, the washed turnips tops and the slices of pork. Season and simmer for another 5–6 minutes. Serve in big bowls.

WINES

A straightforward Rioja from the Tempranillo grape, with a bit of oak, suits this very peasant-style stew. Equally bold is a Corbières. Or for an in-your-face, lip-smacking, traditional wine, try a Hunter Valley Shiraz.

RIOJA
CORBIÈRES
AUSTRALIAN HUNTER VALLEY SHIRAZ

SERVES 6

1.2kg pork shoulder, boned
3 garlic cloves, peeled
2 onions, peeled and sliced
1kg potatoes (Ratte, Rosevale or Charlotte)
3 spicy cooking chorizo sausages, about 60g each
600g turnips tops, washed
salt and pepper

Scotch-style Lamb Stew

This is the kind of meal you need after being out all day, battling with the elements. As with all braised dishes, this is better re-heated and eaten the next day, so make it in advance if you can.

SERVES 6
180g pearl barley
600g boned middle neck of
   lamb, cut into 3cm cubes
salt and pepper
1 large carrot
2 sticks of celery,
1 large onion
4 medium-size turnips
1 bunch of parsley,
   chopped

Rinse the barley in cold water and leave to drain. Cover the lamb with about 2 litres of cold water, season and bring to the boil. Skim well, then simmer gently for 45 minutes.

Meanwhile wash and peel the vegetables and cut into small dice. When the 45 minutes are up, add the barley and diced vegetables to the pot and simmer for 30–40 minutes longer, until everything is tender. You may need to top up the liquid from time to time with boiling water. Add the chopped parsley and serve with boiled potatoes on a cold winter day.

If you're not eating this right away, chill it quickly and refrigerate until needed. To reheat, place in a thick-bottomed pan, bring to the boil and cook until heated through and piping hot.

WINES
A sweet ale works wonders. And a classy second-growth St Julien, such as Gruaud Larose, will certainly raise a smile north of the border, until they have to pay for it!

STOUT OR SWEET ALE
ARGENTINIAN TEMPRANILLO
ST JULIEN BORDEAUX
NEW ZEALAND PINOT NOIR

Boiled Leg of Mutton with Anchovy and Parsley Sauce

How tastes have changed over the years. Mutton is the meat of sheep more than two years old, and in my view, we should go back to this traditional meat and the way of farming it stands for. You can buy mutton from specialist producers and from Halal butchers.

Cover the leg of mutton with water and bring to the boil. Skim, then add the prepared vegetables, bay leaves, spice, parsley and seasoning. Turn down to a very gentle simmer, and cook for about 2½ hours or until tender. Leave to cool in the liquid for at least 2 hours. It will still be just the right temperature for eating. Carve the lamb at the table and serve with the sauce.

Sauce Skim off and strain some of the fat on the top of the lamb cooking pot. Use 4 tablespoons of this tasty fat to sweat the onions until tender. Add the flour and stir in well. Over a high heat, gradually pour in 300ml of the cooking liquid from the mutton and mix well to avoid any lumps. Add the cream and simmer for 5 minutes. Just before serving the lamb, season the sauce with a generous amount of white pepper and add the parsley, chopped anchovies and lemon juice.

WINES

In good years, Chinon ages beautifully to a rich complex red that has just the right balance for mutton and this slightly salty sauce. The Musar from Lebanon has had its highs and lows, but is still a good wine for this strong-flavoured meat.

OLD CHINON

CHÂTEAU MUSAR

CALIFORNIAN ZINFANDEL

SERVES 10–12

1 leg of mutton, about 3.5kg

2 sticks of celery

2 onions, peeled and cut into quarters

1 leek, trimmed and cut into quarters

2 bay leaves

1 tbsp allspice berries

a handful of parsley stalks

salt

Sauce

4 tbsp lamb fat

2 onions, peeled and chopped

1 heaped tbsp plain flour

250ml single cream

ground white pepper

1 bunch of parsley, coarsely chopped

20 good-quality anchovies in oil, rinsed and coarsely chopped

juice of 2 lemons

Red Onion, Fennel and Chilli Tarte Tatin

My wife Gisele makes this vegetable version of a French classic wonderfully well. I consider myself very lucky if there's any left for me to nibble on when I come in at one in the morning after a long day at work.

SERVES 4

220g puff pastry

6 red onions

3 fennel bulbs

4 mild red chillies

100ml olive oil

2 tbsp balsamic vinegar

1 tsp coriander seeds, crushed

salt and pepper

60g caster sugar

2 tsp thyme leaves

3 garlic cloves, crushed

100g grated Parmesan

Roll out the pastry into a circle large enough to cover a tart tin or tatin dish of about 20cm in diameter. Place the pastry in the fridge to rest until needed.

Preheat the oven to 190°C/gas 5. Peel the onions and slice into thick rounds. Remove the outer sections of the fennel and cut each bulb into 6 pieces, removing some of the core. Take the stalks off the chillies but leave them whole. Put all these vegetables into a roasting pan, pour over the olive oil and balsamic vinegar and add the crushed coriander seeds, salt and pepper. Roast in the hot oven for 30 minutes, turning occasionally but being careful to keep the onion rings in one piece. In a separate pan, or directly in the tatin dish, mix the sugar with 3 tablespoons of water. Quickly bring them to the boil and cook, without stirring, until golden brown. Take off the heat and pour into the base of the tart tin if you've used a separate pan.

Turn the oven up to 200°C/gas 6. Arrange all the vegetables in a decorative pattern in the tin and press down tight. Sprinkle with the thyme, garlic and Parmesan. Cover with the puff pastry and tuck in at the edges between the vegetables and the sides of the tin. Prick the pastry with a fork and bake at for 30—40 minutes, until the puff pastry is golden and fully cooked. Leave to cool for at least 20 minutes before turning upside down onto a serving dish so the vegetables, with their caramel topping, are sitting on the crispy pastry.

WINES

The fruit beer from Belgium is delicious with a slightly spicy sweet dish like this. However, a medium white from Kent, with a blend of Seyval Blanc and Müller-Thurgau, is equally good. If you prefer a red, look no further than a good rosé from a Grenache grape.

KRIEK BELGIAN BEER

MEDIUM WHITE ENGLISH WINE

GRENACHE ROSÉ

Stuffed Nan Bread
with Lentils and Spinach

Mildly spicy, these little Indian sandwiches are best served hot. However, they're also good cold for a picnic, served with mango chutney or a curry-scented mayonnaise.

Mix the flour, salt and 2 tablespoons of ghee with 250ml water to make a firm dough. Knead for at least 10 minutes – this can be done with a dough hook attachment in a mixing machine. Shape the dough into a ball, cover with a damp cloth and leave to rest for at least 1 hour.

Rinse the lentils in cold water. Put in a pan, cover with water and simmer for 15 minutes or until cooked. Add the spinach and once it's cooked – a matter of seconds – remove from the pan and drain in a sieve until dry.

In another pan warm up the remaining 2 tablespoons of ghee and add the spices. Stir well and cook until the mustard seeds start to pop and release their flavour. Add the onion and garlic, cook for 2–3 minutes longer, then add the drained lentil mix. Check seasoning and leave to cool.

Preheat the oven to 220°C/gas 7. Divide the dough into 12 and shape into balls. Lightly dust with flour and roll out into rounds about 12cm in diameter. Place some of the lentil mix in the centre of each round, then fold over, pressing the edges well to seal. Flatten the rounds very lightly with a rolling pin or gently press them out with your hands. Brush with a little more ghee and bake in the hot oven for 15 minutes, until crisp and puffed.

WINES

India Pale Ale is high in alcohol and bitterness from hops and a good accompaniment to this dish. Served lightly chilled, both the Zinfandel and the Beaujolais have fruity overtones that match this spicy sandwich well.

INDIA PALE ALE
CALIFORNIAN ZINFANDEL
YOUNG FRESH BEAUJOLAIS

SERVES 6
500g wholewheat flour
2 tsp salt
4 tbsp ghee, plus a little
  more for brushing
200g lentils (brown or red)
500g spinach, washed
2 tsp ground cumin
2 tsp black mustard seeds
1 tsp chilli powder
1 onion finely chopped
2 garlic cloves, peeled and
  crushed

Fine Wines
Usually you choose a wine to go with the food you are serving, but sometimes when you have a special bottle you will want to plan the menu around it. Here are some suggestions for very fine wines and dishes to complement them.

SASSICAIA 1990
TENUTA SAN GUIDO

This is a superb Tuscan Cabernet. Silky smooth with truffle overtones, it is one of the world's great wines and can be drunk with most meats. But with a dish like this, who needs meat?

Truffled Macaroni

SERVES 4

400g large macaroni

320g button mushrooms, cleaned and finely chopped

2 shallots, peeled and finely chopped

1 tbsp butter

120g mascarpone

180g dry white breadcrumbs

2 whole eggs

salt and pepper

nutmeg

100g grated Parmesan cheese

100g cooked black truffle, chopped

Bring plenty of salted water to the boil and cook the macaroni until 'al dente'. Drain and set aside.

Sweat the chopped mushrooms and shallots in a wide pan with the butter until all the moisture has evaporated. Add the mascarpone and continue to cook for 3 minutes, stirring well. Take off the heat and stir in the breadcrumbs, beaten eggs, salt, pepper, nutmeg and a little of the Parmesan. Finally, add the chopped truffle.

Preheat the oven to 190°C/gas 5. Put the mixture into a piping bag and push some into each of the macaroni. Place the filled macaroni in a lightly buttered oven dish. Sprinkle with the rest of the Parmesan and bake for 12–15 minutes until golden and cooked through.

Adding truffles is extravagant but worth it. This dish can be made without them, though, using an equivalent amount of shitake mushrooms instead.

CHASSAGNE-MONTRACHET MORGEOT PREMIER CRU JEAN NOEL GAGNARD 1999

This white Burgundian beauty is dry yet rich, almost textured. It's designed to be aged five years or more. The nutty flavour of the buttered turbot will mirror the wine and the rich buttery sauce is a classic gastronomic treat.

Roast Turbot

SERVES 6

6 thick T-bones of turbot,
  each weighing 280g.
  You'll need a fish
  weighing about 4kg
flour for dredging
salt and pepper
30ml olive oil
3 tbsp of butter
4 shallots, peeled and
  chopped
knob of butter
100ml dry white wine
1 bay leaf
125ml double cream
160g cold butter, diced
salt and pepper
lemon juice to taste

Ask your fishmonger to cut and skin the fish for you. Season the flour and lightly dust the pieces of fish. Heat the oil in a large enough pan to take all the fish comfortably. When the oil is smoking, place the fish in the pan followed by the 3 tablespoons of butter. Continue to cook over a high heat until the butter is foaming, then reduce the heat a little. After 4–5 minutes turn the fish over and continue to cook until equally golden on the other side. Using a spoon, baste the fish with the foaming butter several times. Gently take out of the pan and leave to rest for another 4–5 minutes in a warm place.

Discard the fat in the pan and add the chopped shallots and a knob of fresh butter. Cook for a couple of minutes, then deglaze the pan with the white wine. Add the bay leaf and reduce by half then pour in the cream. Bring to the boil and whisk in the butter a little at a time. Pass through a fine sieve, season and add a few drops of lemon juice if needed. Serve with the turbot.

CHÂTEAU-CHALON 1955 JEAN BOURDY

This unusual wine from the Jura region is actually not a château but an appellation controllé. This wine comes in strange-shaped bottles of 62cl. It is made from the little known Savagnin grape and aged in barrels for a minimum of six years. It develops a floating crust, which gives it its distinctive dry sherry flavour, but with an almost floral note.

Chicken and Cashew Nut Curry

Place the ginger and garlic in a blender with 125ml of water, 1 green chilli, turmeric and 80g of the cashew nuts. In a small pan with a drizzle of ghee fry the coriander seeds, clove and a little black pepper until they start to pop. Add the seeds to the blender and blitz everything until smooth. Set aside.

Cut the chicken into eight pieces and fry until golden all over in a large saucepan with some of the ghee. Remove and drain. Fry the onions in the same pan until lightly coloured. Put back the chicken, season with salt, then pour on the spice mix. Add another 225ml of water and bring to a very gentle simmer. Cover with greaseproof paper and continue to cook for 45 minutes, turning and stirring occasionally. Just before serving, pour in the yoghurt and simmer for a further 2—3 minutes. Slice the second chilli and gently roast the remaining nuts. Sprinkle the chilli, nuts and chopped coriander over the chicken, check the seasoning and serve immediately.

SERVES 4

30g fresh root ginger, peeled and roughly chopped
2 garlic cloves, peeled and roughly chopped
2 green chillies
2 heaped tsp turmeric
180g unsalted cashew nuts
3 tbsp ghee or clarified butter (can be replaced by vegetable oil)
1 tsp coriander seeds
1 clove
black pepper
1 corn-fed chicken, about 1.6kg
2 medium onions, peeled and sliced
salt
125ml natural yoghurt
1 bunch of fresh coriander, chopped
salt and pepper

VEGA-SICILIA
COSECHA 1989 "UNICO"

Made from Tinto fino or Tempranillo grapes, this great spicy red from the Ribera del Duero region is best aged 10 years or more. It can have a high alcohol content, but don't be put off — it is a masterpiece of winemaking.

Roast Snipe

SERVES 4

8 snipe

4 brioche slices, cut 1cm
  thick by 4cm long

butter and oil for frying

1 tbsp duck fat or pork fat

2 chicken livers

3 shallots, peeled and
  chopped

30ml brandy

160g cooked foie gras

salt and pepper

4 tbsp butter

2 tbsp olive oil

200ml white chicken stock
  (see page 32)

Using a pair of tweezers and a damp cloth remove any feathers left from the regular plucking of the snipe and remove feathers from the head. Take out the eyes and windpipe and discard. Make a small incision at the rear and carefully remove all the entrails. Press gently on the entrails to find the gizzard, which will be hard. Remove and discard this as it is full of gravel.

Fry the slices of brioche in a little olive oil and butter. Set aside. Place the duck fat in a pan over high heat and add the entrails, chicken livers and shallots. Season well and add a splash of the brandy. Cook briefly, a minute or less — the livers should be very pink. While still warm, press everything through a fine sieve and beat with a spoon to amalgamate. The mixture should be like a smooth liver pâté. Divide this between the brioche slices.

Divide the cooked foie gras into eight pieces and push one into each snipe. Season the birds and truss in the traditional way by putting the beak through the thigh. Heat 2 tablespoons of butter and 2 tablespoons of oil until foaming. The fat should be so hot that when you add the snipe it froths up over them, covering the birds. Turn the snipe often so they cook and brown evenly. They should take no more than 7–8 minutes for pink meat. Remove and set aside to rest and drain.

Discard the cooking butter and over high heat, stir in the remaining shallots. After a few seconds, pour in the rest of the brandy followed by the chicken stock. Reduce by half and then whisk in 2 tablespoons of butter to thicken and shine the sauce. Warm the brioche croutons in the oven (150°C/gas 2) for 5–6 minutes to re-heat. Remove the heads of the snipe and cut in half following the line of the beak to reveal the delicious little brain. Serve the birds on the croutons with a few roast potatoes and mushrooms.

OPUS ONE, MONDAVI-ROTHSCHILD NAPA VALLEY 1989

*'It isn't Mouton and it isn't Mondavi', said Robert Mondavi.
This is a Bordeaux-style blend made from Cabernet Sauvignon, Merlot
and Cabernet Franc grapes — a full-bodied and sophisticated luxury.*

Peppered Haunch of Venison

SERVES 8

1 haunch of venison, about
    1.6kg, skinned and
    trimmed
2 tbsp cracked white and
    black peppercorns
salt
2–3 tbsp olive oil
200g butter
3 shallots, peeled
2 sticks of celery
1 carrot, peeled
1 sprig of thyme
1 bay leaf
brandy
300ml dark strong red wine
1 tbsp redcurrant jelly
4 tbsp red wine vinegar
500ml veal stock
    (see page 53)
1 tbsp crushed green
    peppercorns

Ask your supplier for venison that has been hung for 10–14 days in its skin. Once it has been trimmed and skinned, rub with the cracked black and white peppercorns, salt and a little oil. Set aside for 20 minutes so the mixture can permeate before the meat is cooked.

Preheat the oven to 200°C/gas 6. In a hot roasting pan evenly colour the haunch on each side in the oil and half the butter. Add the vegetables, thyme and bay leaf, and roast in the oven for 35–40 minutes. Baste occasionally and turn once. To check whether the meat is done, push a barding needle into the centre for a few seconds and remove. It should be lukewarm for pink meat. Leave in a warm place to rest for 20–30 minutes before slicing.

Drain all the fat out of the pan but keep the vegetables. Over high heat add a little brandy to deglaze the pan, then add the wine, jelly and red wine vinegar. Boil, scraping the bottom of the tray well to lift off the roasting sugars, until the liquid is reduced by two thirds. Then add the stock and reduce again by half. Pass through a fine sieve and add any juices that have run from the venison. Whisk in the remaining cold butter and crushed green peppercorns and serve with the venison.

PENFOLDS GRANGE HERMITAGE 1975

This is a dish that needs a classy wine with attitude. Grange is deep purple in colour with a boldness that belies its age. I shall always remember my first taste back in 1983 — 90 per cent Shiraz, 10 per cent Cabernet Sauvignon. Bonza! It's almost impossible to find this particular vintage, but choose one that is at least 15 years old.

Roast Saddle of Hare with Red Wine and Mustard Velouté

Ask your butcher to trim the hare and remove the sinews, but be sure to take these with the meat. Place the trimmings and sinews in a wide saucepan with the olive oil, chopped garlic and the brown sugar and caramelise over a high heat. When the meat starts to colour, turn down the heat a little and add a tablespoon of butter — keep the butter frothing. Add the juniper, bay, thyme and sliced onion. When the onion has also browned, drain off the fat and pour in the wine. Bring to a simmer, skim and reduce until sticky and almost dry. Add the veal stock and reduce by half. Pass this through a fine sieve pressing well. Set aside.

Preheat the oven to 200°C/mark 6. Season the saddles and sear in a roasting tray with oil and most of the rest butter (reserve 1 tablespoon) until evenly coloured. Roast for 12 minutes, basting occasionally. Take out and leave to rest for 15 minutes in a warm place before carving.

Drain the fat from the tray and pour in the brandy, Crème de Cassis and port. Bring to the boil, then pass through a fine sieve into the first sauce made with the trimmings. To finish the sauce, bring to the boil, then add the cream and simmer for 5–6 minutes. Whisk in a tablespoon of butter and the mustard, then check the seasoning. Serve with the hare.

SERVES 4

2 hare saddles, 800g each, trimmed of all sinews
2 tbsp olive oil
2 garlic cloves, peeled and chopped
2 tsp soft brown sugar
100g butter
5 juniper berries, crushed
1 bay leaf
1 sprig of thyme
1 onion, peeled and sliced
300ml strong dark red wine, Syrah/Shiraz
200ml veal stock (see page 53)
salt and pepper
olive oil
2 tbsp brandy
2 tbsp Crème de Cassis
2 tbsp port
150ml double cream
1 tbsp Dijon mustard

VOSNE-ROMANÉE CROS-PARENTOUX HENRI JAYER 1993

Pinot Noir at its best — simple, straightforward, with grilled beef to bring out the best of the Burgundian icon. With age, a good Burgundy takes on an almost vegetal scent, quite astonishing and complex.

Grilled Rib of Beef

SERVES 4

2 ribs of beef, about 350g
  each
olive oil
salt and pepper

There is no secret to a good rib of beef. To me, it's obvious that if you buy beef from a small farm (not necessarily organic, although most are) that takes care of its animals and feeds and breeds them properly, you have a good chance of enjoying a fine piece of meat. The meat should be well hung — four weeks in my view.

The easy bit is the cooking and a grilled rib is quite simply delicious. I am not keen on gas-fired barbecues and there is no substitute for 'sarmant de vignes' as they say in Bordeaux. Vine cuttings and small logs from old vines give a certain flavour to the beef that is delicate and at the same time quite distinctive. I appreciate it may be difficult to find a vineyard in England prepared to hand over these tasty twigs, so try using a good flavoursome hard wood, such as oak, hazel or cherry, instead.

Rub the trimmed ribs with a little olive oil, salt and pepper, then set on the grill over a medium heat. This is a thick cut of meat so needs to cook slowly. Turn so that it cooks and marks evenly. The beef should take 20 minutes for medium rare. Don't forget to let it rest for at least 10 minutes in a warm place before carving.

GRAND VIN DE CHÂTEAU LATOUR 1982

A Pauillac is more often paired with lamb, but to be honest, a wine of this character — especially an '82 — needs a meat with a little more structure and less nose. All Pauillacs need at least ten years to be at their best before you can even think about drinking them.

Roast Rib of Veal

SERVES 4

800—900g trimmed rib of
    veal, remove the
    backbone and French
    trim; tie with butcher's
    string
salt and pepper
4 tbsp vegetable oil
2 tbsp butter
1 onion, peeled and
    chopped
1 carrot, peeled and
    chopped
1 stick of celery, chopped
1 garlic clove, peeled and
    chopped

Creamed pasta
160g pasta
8 white button mushrooms
180ml double cream
1 tbsp crème fraîche
salt and pepper
80g Emmental cheese,
    grated

Rub the veal with salt and pepper. In a roasting tray just the right size for the veal, preferably a cocotte (cast-iron roasting pot), heat the oil until it's hot enough to sear the veal on all sides. Add the butter and roughly chopped vegetables and put in the oven at 180°C/gas 4 for 30 minutes, turning it twice. Remove the veal, cover lightly and leave in a warm place to rest. Remove the vegetables and set aside.

Drain off as much fat as possible and return the pan to a hot stove, stirring and scraping the bottom for 2—3 minutes. Pour on 300ml of water and continue to stir and reduce this natural jus for 3—4 minutes. Add in the juices that have run off the veal and press through a fine sieve. Serve this with the veal and roasted vegetables. Creamed pasta is also a good accompaniment.

Creamed pasta I find coquillettes or little shell-shaped pasta works well, but any shape that has a cavity to hold sauce is fine. Cook the pasta in boiling salted water until tender. Rinse and drain well, shaking the colander to remove all the water.

Wash the mushrooms and chop them very finely. Put them in a pan with the double cream and simmer until the liquid is reduced by half. Gently fold in the pasta, crème fraîche and seasoning. Pour the mixture into an ovenproof dish, sprinkle with the cheese and glaze under a hot grill for a few minutes.

MORGENHOF ESTATE PREMIÈRE SÉLECTION 1999

The Stellenbosch Estate consistently produces beautifully complex Bordeaux blend-style wines that are astoundingly good. French-owned and made by ladies, this is a seriously sexy wine.

Roast Leg of Lamb with Rosemary and Garlic

SERVES 6–8
24 small new potatoes
1 leg of lamb, 1.8–2kg
3 tbsp olive oil
salt and pepper
2 heads of garlic
2 sprigs of rosemary
2 tbsp butter
24 pearl onions, peeled
200ml dry white wine
knob of butter

Peel the new potatoes. Parboil for 3 minutes in salted water, drain and set aside.

Preheat the oven to 200°C/gas 6. Rub the leg of lamb with a little oil, salt and pepper. Peel 3 cloves of garlic and cut in half lengthways. Make six incisions in the leg of lamb and insert a piece of garlic and a small piece of rosemary into each one. Break up the rest of the garlic without peeling. Place the lamb in a hot roasting tray with the rest of the oil and sear over a medium heat until golden on all sides. Add the butter and continue to heat until foaming. Put the parboiled potatoes, pearl onions, and the rest of the garlic and rosemary into the foaming butter around the lamb. Season and put in the oven for 10 minutes. Turn the potatoes and onions occasionally and baste the lamb with the fat. Turn the oven down to 190°C/gas 5 and continue to cook for 45–60 minutes.

Take the meat and vegetables out of the pan and keep warm. Pour out most of the fat and add the wine, followed by 200ml of water. Bring to the boil and scrape the tray with a spatula to lift the roasting sugars. Continue to boil and add any juices that have run from the leg of lamb. When reduced by half, whisk in a knob of butter, then pass the sauce through a fine sieve. Serve with the lamb and vegetables.

Cheese

In my view, there are very few cheeses that go well with red wine. The deep-rooted belief that red wine and cheese are the perfect match should be well and truly forgotten. Even my wife will often say, 'Let's have some cheese to finish the red wine', and then choose a selection of goat cheese that would be better off with a crisp Sauvignon Blanc.

Cheese is probably the easiest food to experiment with in terms of taste and how wines and food interact with each other. Next time you choose a selection of cheese in a restaurant, don't eat them in the order the stuffy maître d'hôtel tells you to. Instead, try little pieces and take a sip of your wine after each. Decide which one goes best with the wine and finish with that. As you will soon find out, some matches are made in heaven, while others leave your mouth feeling like you have bitten into a piece of willow bark with a spoonful of washing-up liquid for good measure! Cooked cheese dishes make different demands, so here are my suggestions.

Quinta do Noval Vintage Port 1963
This is one of the finest years for this port. Aged in the bottle, it has a lovely colour, a nutty flavour and aromas of liquorice and toffee, which go well with blue cheeses and very mature Cheddars.

Cheese Charlotte with Balsamic Dressing

A good way to use up pieces of cheese left over after a dinner party. Don't serve this too cold or the texture will be hard.

SERVES 8

125g blue cheese (Roquefort, Oxford, Cashel)

125g moist goat cheese (Buche, Pyramide, Ragstone)

125g strong soft cow's cheese (Livarot, Maroilles, Stinking Bishop)

75g butter

2 shallots, peeled and finely chopped

2 sprigs of tarragon and chervil, roughly chopped

1 bunch of chives, roughly chopped

140ml whipping cream

1 celery heart, cut into sticks

5 tbsp strong olive oil

2 tbsp good aged balsamic vinegar

salt and pepper

Put all the cheeses with the butter in a food processor and blitz until smooth. Beat in the shallots and some of the roughly chopped herbs, keeping some aside to sprinkle on top.

Whisk the cream until it forms peaks and fold into the cheese mix. Gently pour this into ramekins or into rings, about 4 x 3cm in size, placed on a baking sheet. Level off the surface and cover with clingfilm. Refrigerate for at least 3 hours.

To serve, run a small hot knife around the edges of the ring and gently remove. To make the dressing, mix together the olive oil, balsamic vinegar and seasoning. Dress the celery sticks and serve with the cheese charlottes.

WINES

The choice of wine depends to some extent on the combination of cheeses, but fragrant whites, such as Gewürztraminer and Grüner Veltliner, with a good level of acidity, work really well. Beaujolais Villages, made from the gulpable Gamay grape, is the red of choice.

GEWÜRZTRAMINER
GRÜNER VELTLINER
BEAUJOLAIS VILLAGES

Potato and Apple Pancake with Melted Gorgonzola

This is a delicious and easy way to enjoy this particularly creamy blue cheese. The apple flavour with the cheese is a mouth-watering combination.

Peel the potatoes and grate on a coarse cheese grater. Do the same with the apples. Season with a little salt, pepper and nutmeg, add a few rosemary leaves, then place the apples and potatoes in a clean cloth and squeeze to remove excess moisture.

Add the crème fraîche and egg yolks, and mix well. Heat a little olive oil and butter in a non-stick pan until foaming. Spoon in some mixture to make a pancake about 6cm wide and 0.5cm thick. Cook gently for 4–5 minutes, then using a pallet knife, flip over to cook on the other side. The pancake should be golden brown and crisp. Repeat to make 8 pancakes.

Place 4 pancakes on an ovenproof dish. Crumble the cheese over them and place in the oven at 180°C/gas 4 until the cheese begins to melt. Take out and top each one with another pancake. Serve with the apricot and walnut vinaigrette drizzled at the side.

Apricot and walnut vinaigrette Coarsely chop the walnuts and apricots. Add the oil, vinegar, honey, salt and pepper and mix well.

WINES
Port goes well with apples – in fact, Cox apples and Tawny Port are a classic combination. A Maury, from southwest France, is also a good choice.

TAWNY PORT
MAURY

SERVES 4
2 large Desirée or Maris
  Piper potatoes
2 Cox apples
salt and pepper
nutmeg
2 sprigs of rosemary
1 tbsp crème fraîche
2 egg yolks
1 tbsp vegetable oil
2 tsp butter
260g Gorgonzola

Apricot and walnut
vinaigrette
12 walnut halves
4 dried apricots
3 tbsp walnut oil
1 tbsp red wine vinegar
1 tsp clear honey
salt and pepper

Cheese and Ham Fritters

The tried-and-tested cheese and ham combination always comes up trumps.

MAKES 20 PIECES
200g semi-hard cheese,
   such as Mimolette or
   Emmental
6 thin slices of cooked ham
   cut into strips
150ml lager
2 eggs, separated
80g plain flour, sifted
1 pinch of salt
vegetable oil for deep frying

Cut the cheese into cubes, 2 x 2cm. Wrap each cube in a strip of ham and hold in place with a wooden cocktail stick.

Whisk together the lager, egg yolks, flour and salt until smooth. Whisk the egg whites and fold them into the mixture. Heat the vegetable oil in a deep fryer or large pan. Dip the cheese and ham cubes into the batter and deep fry. Serve immediately.

WINES
If this is served as an aperitif or snack, a refreshing lager may be the perfect accompaniment. Otherwise, try a Rosé Champagne, which has a bit more body than a white. Even a touch of sweetness can work with these tasty morsels — something like a medium sweet German Spätlese.

WHITE LAGER
ROSÉ CHAMPAGNE
RHINE RIESLING SPÄTLESE

Deep-fried Almond-coated Camembert

This recipe is a throwback to the 80s, but if made with good Camembert it's a real treat. The cheese is rolled in choux pastry, which makes a lovely crisp coating.

Cut the Camembert into big bite-size morsels, about 2 x 3cm, keeping the rind on. Leave in the refrigerator.

To make a choux paste, bring 250ml water to the boil with the butter, a pinch of salt and a generous grinding of white pepper. Take off the flame and with a wooden spatula, beat in the flour until smooth. Beat in the eggs one by one – this takes a lot of effort but is well worth the trouble.

Using a wet tablespoon, make a little ball of this paste, push in a piece of Camembert and reshape while still on the spoon. Repeat until all the mixture and cheese is used up. Put in the refrigerator to set for an hour.

Roll the balls in the ground almonds, making sure the cheese is well covered. Heat some vegetable oil in a deep fryer or large pan. Deep fry the almond-coated morsels at 170°C until golden on all sides – about 4–5 minutes. These can be served as a starter or with drinks before a meal.

WINES

The two New World sparklers are refreshing and have a good depth of flavour from careful blending, especially the selected cuvées. The sparkling wine from Saumur has carbon dioxide added, but if you find a well-aged one that's spent a little time in barrels you will be pleasantly surprised. This wine is made mainly from the Chenin grape, with a little Chardonnay.

TASMANIAN SPARKLING WINE
SOUTH AFRICAN SPARKLING WINE
SAUMUR MOUSSEUX

SERVES 6
1 ripe farmhouse
  Camembert
80g butter
salt and white pepper
180g plain flour
3 eggs
200g ground almonds
vegetable oil for deep frying

Hot Goat Cheese Pies with Olives

Rocamadour cheeses are almost small enough to pop into your mouth whole and perfect for making into these little pies. A good starter.

SERVES 8
500g plain flour
60g strong olive oil
1 pinch salt
16 Rocamadour cheeses
  (cheese that is a little dry
  is best)
16 black olives marinated in
  oil, chopped
16 green olives marinated
  in oil, chopped
2 garlic cloves, peeled and
  chopped
1 bunch of basil
1 egg for egg wash

Sift the flour. Make a well, add the oil and 140ml of water, then bring the dough together using your fingertips. Do not overwork. Wrap in clingfilm and refrigerate for an hour.

Roll out the dough using a pasta roller set to 0. Place 8 rings, measuring 5 x 2cm, on a baking sheet. Cut the dough into circles 8cm across and line each ring – you'll find you have a little more dough than you need.

Preheat the oven to 190°C/gas 5. Place a Rocamadour cheese in each lined ring. Add a spoonful of chopped olives and garlic, then a couple of basil leaves. Place another Rocamadour on top of the olives, followed by a couple more basil leaves. Bring the overlapping pastry over the cheese and seal well by pressing and moistening with a little water. Turn the pies over so that the seal is underneath. Brush with beaten egg and score with the point of a knife to decorate. Bake in the oven for 15–20 minutes until golden.

WINES

The classic combo of goat cheese and Sauvignon Blanc needs added 'oomph' because of the olives, hence the pungent Fumé from California or the New Zealand offering. But for something different and exciting, try an up-and-coming white from Greece. This wine comes from hills of Nemea and is made from the indigenous white grapes, Savatiano and Roditis.

CALIFORNIA SAUVIGNON BLANC
NEW ZEALAND SAUVIGNON BLANC
NEMEA, PELOPONNESE WHITE

Pilau Rice with Beaufort Cheese

Look for an old Beaufort made from the summer pastures. Alternatively, you could use a mature Cheddar. The mountain sausage is a dry, thin salami made from pork.

Preheat the oven to 190°C /gas 5. Put the sultanas in a pan, cover with cold water and bring to a simmer for 2 minutes. Drain and set aside. Sweat the onion in a wide pan with a tablespoon of butter until soft but not coloured. Add the cumin, thyme, bay leaf and rice. Stir to coat the rice, cook for two to three minutes, then pour on the chicken stock. Bring to the boil, cover with a greaseproof paper and put in the oven for 16–18 minutes.

Take out and remove the paper. All the liquid should have been absorbed and the rice should be just cooked. With a fork, gently fluff up the rice and mix in the walnuts, sultanas, remaining butter and half of the cheese. Season to taste. Place in a hot bowl and sprinkle with the sausage and remaining cheese.

WINES
The Arbois is from the same region as the Beaufort so it is the obvious first choice. The Macon is a well-rounded Burgundy, without being too expensive, while Fino is always a good match for sausage and mature cheese.

VIN D'ARBOIS
MACON BLANC
FINO SHERRY

SERVES 4

1 tbsp sultanas or golden
  raisins
1 onion, peeled and
  chopped
2 tbsp butter
1 tsp cumin seeds
2 sprigs of thyme
1 bay leaf
200g long-grain rice
500ml white chicken stock
  (see page 32)
12 fresh walnuts, chopped
200g Beaufort cheese, cut
  into shavings with a
  peeler or slicer
salt and pepper
1 mountain sausage, about
  200g, skinned and sliced
  thinly

Hot Pears with Roquefort and Walnuts

Pears, like apples, go well with lots of cheeses because of their sweet and sour taste. This recipe could be eaten as a starter or a cheese course. Double the quantities given if serving as a starter.

SERVES 4

2 ripe pears, Williams
    or Passe-Crassane
120g Roquefort cheese,
    crumbled into pieces
60g walnuts, roughly
    chopped
1 tbsp crème fraîche
1 tbsp port
1 spring onion, sliced
salt and pepper

Take the pears and cut in half lengthways. Remove the seeds and core, then carefully scoop out some of the flesh without splitting the skin. This should leave you with 4 boats.

Roughly chop the pear flesh and add to the crumbled cheese with the walnuts. Fold in the crème fraîche, port, spring onion and seasoning. Fill the boats and bake for 15 minutes at 180°C/gas 4. Put under a hot grill for 2–3 minutes to brown.

WINES

Bonnezeaux is a sweet Loire Valley wine made from the Chenin grape. It's velvety and amber when aged, with a good amount of residual acidity, and served lightly chilled it makes a good partner for blue cheese and walnuts. A medium sweet Oloroso would also be a good match as is the blue cheese stalwart – Tawny Port.

BONNEZEAUX
SWEET OLD OLOROSO SHERRY
TAWNY PORT

Aligot

This speciality is from the Aveyron region of France. It is traditionally made from fresh hard cheese but Lagiole or Cantal can be used instead. This is rich, very rich, and not for dieters or the faint-hearted.

SERVES 6
1kg potatoes, Maris Piper
    or similar
150g butter
200g crème fraîche
350g Tome Fraîche
    d'Auvergne
fresh Cantal or Lagiole
    cheese, crumbled
1 or 2 cloves of garlic,
    finely crushed
salt and pepper

Boil the potatoes in their skins in salted water. When cooked, leave them to cool a little, then remove from the water and peel. Pass through a ricer or mash while still warm. Over a low flame, beat the butter, crème fraîche and crumbled cheese into the potatoes. Do not overheat or the mixture will separate. Season to taste with the crushed garlic, salt and pepper. Serve hot – the potatoes should be smooth, rich and a little elastic. Good with boiled bacon or gammon.

WINES
Crozes-Hermitage might not be the first wine that comes to mind because of its powerful character, yet it has a subtle freshness that means it is extremely versatile. If you prefer a wine to swig in a more relaxed manner, Beaujolais or Pinot Grigio will certainly fit the bill.

CROZES-HERMITAGE
BEAUJOLAIS VILLAGES
PINOT GRIGIO

Crispy Gruyère Pancakes

These crispy pancakes should be served as soon as they're made and can make a good starter or cheese course. Brique pastry is a North African pancake, now available at good delis, but you could use spring roll sheets.

Lay 4 sheets of brique on a work surface. Lightly brush with olive oil. Cut 4 smaller squares from the remaining brique and place these in the centre of each sheet to help support the filling. Brush with oil.

Preheat the oven to 180°C/gas 4. Mix the Gruyère and crème fraîche. Roughly chop the rocket leaves and add them with the spring onions to the cheese mix. Lightly season the mixture and divide between the sheets of brique. Bring the edges together and tie each parcel with a chive. Trim the tops slightly with scissors and brush again with a little olive oil. Bake in an oven at for 8–10 minutes until golden and crisp. Serve immediately.

This is ideal with a little rocket salad seasoned with a crème fraîche vinaigrette and garnished with shavings of Gruyère.

Crème fraîche vinaigrette Mix all the ingredients together and season to taste.

WINES
Warm cheese dishes are fatty, so a little acidity is welcome in the drinks. If you want a red, avoid heavy, cloying Syrahs and choose a light Chianti. Better still, try a Swiss Chasselas or a rosé from Neuchâtel called Oeil de Perdrix (eye of a partridge).

CHIANTI CLASSICO
SWISS CHASSELAS
SWISS OEIL DE PERDRIX

SERVES 4
6 sheets of brique pastry
   (North African paper-
   thin pancakes)
olive oil
120g Gruyère, grated
1 tbsp crème fraîche
40g wild rocket leaves
2 spring onions, sliced
salt and pepper
chives

Crème fraîche vinaigrette
1 tbsp crème fraîche
1 tbsp olive oil
juice of 1 lemon
1 tbsp water
salt and pepper

Fennel Boats
and Grilled Goat Cheese

Crottins de Chavignol work well for this recipe, but make sure they are not too hard. This can be served as a starter or a cheese course.

SERVES 4

1 large bulb of fennel
2 soft crottin goat cheeses
  or similar
salt and pepper
Piment d'Espellette (dried
  chillies) to taste, chopped
5 tbsp olive oil
juice of 1 lemon
1 bunch of basil

Top and tail the fennel and remove the outer stems. Wash and trim these outer stems and shape into 4 boats. Blanch the boats in boiling salted water until lightly cooked, refresh and drain well. Put half a crottin in each boat. Season with a little salt, pepper and chopped chilli, and drizzle with a little olive oil. Bake in a hot oven, 200°C/gas 6, or under a grill until hot and lightly coloured.

Slice the heart of the fennel very thinly across, using a vegetable slicer. Season with lemon juice, the rest of the olive oil, salt, pepper and finally toss in the basil leaves. Serve this with the fennel boats.

WINES

Goat cheese and Sauvignon Blanc is a classic combination, although the fact that this dish is warm and includes fennel changes the texture and weight. A strong New Zealand Sauvignon will come up trumps, or the sharpness of a Sancerre will help cut through the slightly fatty cheese. For a real change and delight, try an Apremont wine from the Savoie region. This is made from the little-known Jacquère grape.

SAVOIE APREMONT

SANCERRE

MARLBOROUGH SAUVIGNON BLANC

Cashel Blue Cream with Grapes and Grappa

You can use a Fourme d'Ambert instead of Cashel for this dish, but the tangy acidity of the Cashel works well with the grapes and sugar syrup.

Leave the cheese to soften at room temperature. Using a fork, beat in the crème fraîche and lightly season with salt and pepper – the cheese should still be slightly lumpy. Spoon into nice glasses or ramekins.

Heat the butter in a non-stick pan until foaming. Add the grapes and sugar and toss around over medium heat for about 2 minutes. Add the grappa, take off the heat immediately and leave to cool completely. Pour this mixture equally over the ramekins. Serve with toasted wholemeal or soda bread.

WINES

Grappa and Gewürztraminer may not spring to mind with cheese but actually work a treat. The fruit beers make a pleasant change especially if this dish is served as a light meal.

GRAPPA, MARC DE GEWÜRZTRAMINER
GEWÜRZTRAMINER
BELGIAN FRUIT BEER

SERVES 6
360g Cashel blue
120g crème fraîche
salt and pepper
1 tbsp butter
36 white seedless grapes
1 tbsp light brown sugar
3 tbsp grappa

Welsh Rarebit

An ideal savoury snack — and perfect with port.

10 SLICES
10 slices of white bread
30g butter
30g flour
200ml stout
300g mature Cheddar
  cheese, grated
100g Double Gloucester,
  grated
2 tsp English mustard
2 pinches cayenne pepper

Toast the bread on both sides and remove the crusts. Melt the butter in a saucepan and add the flour, stirring all the time, to make a roux. Gently pour on the stout, whisking well to avoid lumps. Bring to the boil and over low heat stir in the grated cheeses, mustard and cayenne pepper. As soon as the cheese has melted, take the pan off the heat — do not boil or the mix will curdle. Leave to cool a little, then spread over the toast. Place under the grill until brown and bubbling.

WINES
At the end of a meal, after a little break, what could be better than a glass of port and this all-time classic savoury — but try explaining that to a Frenchman. If you're eating this as a snack or as part of a meal, a bottle of stout or a dark, plummy Australian Shiraz are good accompaniments.

LBV PORT
OLD ALE OR STOUT
OLD AUSTRALIAN SHIRAZ

Spicy Pear and Walnut Condiment for Blue Cheese

Some cheeses need a little help to give of their best — usually something sweet, spicy and tangy. This condiment works well with strong blue cheeses, such as Gorgonzola, Bleu des Causses, Bleu de Gex or Cashel, as well as with hard cheeses.

Wash and peel the lemon and cut the zest into fine julienne. Blanch the strips twice in boiling water and rinse. Slit the vanilla pod and scrape out the seeds.

Put the pod, seeds and lemon julienne in a pan with the red wine, sugar, cinnamon sticks and chilli strips. Bring to a simmer and add the walnuts and the peeled quartered pears. Simmer for 15 minutes or until tender.

Remove the pears and reduce the liquid until syrupy. Season. Return the pears to the pan and add the red wine vinegar. Chill until needed.

SERVES 6

1 lemon
1 vanilla pod
360ml strong red wine
120g soft brown sugar
2 cinnamon sticks
1 mild red chilli, cut into
   julienne strips
120g walnuts
3 pears, William or Passe-
   Crassane, peeled and
   quartered
salt and pepper
2 tbsp red wine vinegar

Hot Vacherin Cheese with Boiled Potatoes and Dry-cured Ham

This speciality from the Jura region is made from unpasteurised cows milk and is only available from September to March. This way of serving it makes an instant meal with very little fuss or work. Make sure you buy properly aged ham to serve with the cheese. If it doesn't say how long it's been aged it's probably only been in an airing factory for a couple of months, which is nowhere near as good.

Preheat the oven to 175°C/gas 3 to 4. Remove any plastic coverings from the Vacherin Mont d'Or. Put the lid back on the box and wrap in aluminium foil. Bake in the oven for 16 minutes. Leave for 2–3 minutes before unwrapping and serving. Boil the potatoes in their skins and serve hot with the thinly sliced ham and Vacherin. Simply bring the cheese to the table with a big spoon and let everyone help themselves.

WINES

Roussette is the obvious choice as it comes from the same region as the cheese. It's fresh, tasty – even refreshing. The Riesling is equally at home, especially if it's a young one. If you want a red, the Rully will be light enough to let the cheese and ham flavours come through without losing any zing.

SAVOIE ROUSSETTE

ALSACE RIESLING

RULLY RED

SERVES 2

1 Vacherin Mont d'Or, about 500g

8–12 small new potatoes (Charlotte or Belle de Fontenay)

10–12 slices of 24-month dry-cured ham, Iberico or Serrano

Tartiflette

This traditional Savoie dish is a calorie-laden feast to have after a day on the ski slopes.

SERVES 6

1kg potatoes (Estima, Desirée or similar)

260g ventreche or dry-cured bacon

vegetable oil

salt and pepper

500g Reblochon, chopped into pieces

Peel the potatoes and cut into large dice. Wash in cold water, put in a pan of salted water and bring to the boil. Cook for 3 minutes, then drain well.

Cut the ventreche into lardons and put in a large frying pan with a dash of vegetable oil. Gently fry the lardons to render some of the fat, then add the potatoes. Continue to cook for 5–6 minutes, stirring occasionally and scraping the pan if necessary, to give the potatoes a little colour. Season the potatoes and ham, then put in an ovenproof dish. Scatter over the chopped Reblochon and bake in a hot oven at 200°C/gas 6 for 15 minutes. Finish under a hot grill to brown the top.

WINES

St Veran is an almost forgotten Burgundian white. It's lighter tasting than its illustrious neighbour Pouilly-Fuissé, but still has the distinctive style everyone loves – clean tasting with a good finish to match the cured bacon. The aromatic Albarino grape variety makes a magical white from the Galicia region, a perfect foil for the tartiflette. If all else fails, cheese and ham always find a friend in a dry sherry.

ST VERAN

GALICIA ALBARIÑO

FINO SHERRY

Fine Wines
Usually you choose a wine to go with the food you are serving, but sometimes when you have a special bottle you will want to plan the menu around it. Here are some suggestions for very fine wines and dishes to complement them.

CHÂTEAU D'YQUEM 1967 LUR SALUCES

Château d'Yquem is more often paired with foie gras, but for me this is not the best of marriages. Use a young vintage if you must. I think the perfect match for this outstanding wine is Roquefort cheese, preferably a rich creamy variety such as Baragnaudes from Société. The creaminess matches the viscosity of the wine — that's easy to understand. But the harsh saltiness and power of the cheese with the sweetness of the wine is harder for some people to fathom. That is, until they've tried it. Both are giants of strength and character. Put them together and heaven could not be smoother or more tender. Alternatively, if you want to drink your Château d'Yquem with something sweet, serve with some Cannelés Bordelais (see page 162).

Roquefort
Roquefort must be served at room temperature. Always take out it out of the fridge a couple of hours before you want to eat, and leave it covered with a damp cloth to prevent it drying out. The partnership of the cheese and wine is sublime. If you want to serve anything else, walnut and raisin bread or plain oatcakes both work well.

Desserts

At this stage of the meal I feel that quality is much more important than quantity and a small glass of sweet wine is enough. In fact, I sometimes go without dessert and just sip the wine instead – although I might want a little more than just a small glass!

When choosing wine for desserts, think of similarities. Sweet Madeiras have coffee, milk, chocolate and nutty tones, so match well to dishes with those flavours. Muscats tend to be fruity so are good partners for desserts containing fresh or dried fruits – Asti Spumante is just right with fresh berries and biscuits. There are exceptions, but as a rule the wine should always be as sweet as the dessert, or even sweeter, for a perfect balance.

Sauternes, one of my favourite sweet wines, is made from Sémillon grapes that have been affected by a mould called *Botrytis cinerea* (noble rot). When this happens, the grapes shrivel and the sugar becomes concentrated. During the wine-making process, not all the sugar is allowed to ferment into alcohol, giving a high residual sugar level and producing a deliciously sweet golden elixir.

Château de la Fonvieille Monbazillac 1945
This famous dessert wine from the Dordogne was made by women during the war years. Lighter than Sauternes, it is usually drunk as a young wine, but a good year, such as this, will keep well. It goes beautifully with caramelised dishes such as Tarte Tatin and with roasted or poached fruits.

Poached Pears with Gingerbread and Pralines

Pink pralines are a speciality of Lyon. You can use plain brown ones instead but the colourful Lyonnais variety do finish the dish well.

SERVES 8
500g caster sugar
250ml white wine
cinnamon stick
2 vanilla pods, split
8 William pears, peeled and
  cored
8 slices of gingerbread for
  serving

Caramel
200g caster sugar
410g evaporated milk,
  unsweetened
200g pink pralines

Sabayon
1 egg yolk
1 whole egg
50g caster sugar
1 leaf of gelatine
65ml Poire William
  liqueur
330ml double cream

Mix the sugar, wine, cinnamon and vanilla in a pan with 1 litre of water. Bring to the boil and simmer for 15 minutes. Add the pears to the syrup and poach until tender. Remove the pears and set aside. Reserve the poaching syrup.

Caramel Mix the sugar with 500ml of water in a pan and cook to a caramel (174°C). This should take about 20 minutes. When done, dip the bottom of the pan in cold water to stop the cooking process. Whisk in the milk and the coarsely crushed pralines.

Sabayon Whisk the eggs and sugar to a ribbon consistency. Soak the gelatine in cold water to soften. Warm the alcohol and dissolve the gelatine in it. Whip the cream to a light, fluffy consistency. Mix the alcohol and gelatine into the eggs, then fold in the cream and leave to set in the fridge.

Serving Place the slices of gingerbread on the plates and lightly soak with the poaching syrup. Slice and fan out the pears and arrange on top of the gingerbread. Mix the sabayon gently into the caramel, pour over the pears and serve.

WINES
Most sweet white wines would go well with this dessert, but the flowery Muscat and the sticky Australian 'noble rot' are both excellent partners. The Vin de Paille, so-called because the grapes are dried on hay before being pressed to concentrate the flavours and sugars, can be quite a revelation.

MUSCAT DE BEAUMES-DE-VENISE
AUSTRALIAN BOTRYTIS SÉMILLON
ARBOIS VIN DE PAILLE

Orange and Poppy Seed Shortbread

This simple recipe has everything a dessert needs — it's creamy, sweet, sharp and crunchy. The shortbread keeps well in an airtight container for several days.

Mix the egg yolk with the crème fraîche and orange zest. With your fingertips, gently incorporate the flour, sugar, poppy seeds and soft butter, but do not knead or overwork the dough. Wrap the dough in clingfilm and refrigerate for 3 hours.

Preheat the oven to 180°C/gas 4. Lightly flour a work surface and roll the dough out to a thickness of 2–3mm. Cut into 12 equal rectangles and place these on a non-stick baking sheet. Bake for about 15 minutes until light brown and cooked through. Leave to cool completely.

Segment the oranges and douse with the Cointreau. Whisk the double cream, crème fraîche and icing sugar until firm. Divide this equally between six plates along with the oranges and shortbread biscuits. Decorate with a little orange peel confit.

Orange peel confit Peel the orange, making sure there is no white pith, and cut into julienne strips. Blanch 3 times in boiling water. Put in a pan with just enough water to cover and add the caster sugar. Simmer until tender and translucent. Remove and cool.

WINES
Barsac, the racy, youthful neighbour of Sauternes, is a match for this fruity dessert, especially if it's a young vintage. If you prefer something more perfumed and a little sweeter, go for an Orange Muscat. Otherwise, a small iced Cointreau is naughty but nice.

BARSAC
CALIFORNIAN ORANGE MUSCAT
ICED COINTREAU

SERVES 6
1 egg yolk
1 tbsp crème fraîche
zest of 1 orange
250g plain flour
60g caster sugar
2 tbsp poppy seeds
60g salted butter

Filling
6 oranges
2 tbsp Cointreau
200ml double cream
1 tbsp crème fraîche
100g icing sugar

Orange peel confit
1 orange
3 tbsp caster sugar

Lemon Pie

This is a rustic beauty that will please all you lemon lovers. It is delicious with custard or a big spoonful of crème fraîche.

SERVES 6

Pastry
1 egg
1 tbsp cream
30g caster sugar
200g butter
400g plain flour
100g ground almonds
1 pinch salt

Filling
3 lemons washed
450g caster sugar
3 eggs
100g demerara sugar
2 heaped tbsp mascarpone

Pastry Mix the egg, cream and sugar. Gently incorporate the butter, flour, almonds and salt with your fingertips, but do not overwork the dough. Wrap in clingfilm and put in the fridge to rest for 30 minutes. Roll out two sheets of dough to fit a 20cm tart ring. Butter the tart ring and place on a sheet of greaseproof paper on a baking sheet. Line the tart ring with one sheet of dough, leaving some overlapping.

Filling Cut the lemons in half lengthways, then slice across as thinly as possible. Put the lemon slices in a bowl with any juice that has run, add the caster sugar and gently mix. Cover and leave to marinate for 12 hours.

Preheat the oven to 230°C/gas 8. Whisk the eggs, demerara sugar and mascarpone together and add to the lemons. Pour the filling into the lined tart tin and cover with the other sheet of dough. Press down the edges to seal and cut off any excess pastry with a knife. Make a small hole in the centre to let out steam. Bake for 10 minutes at 230°C/gas 8, then turn down to 200°C/gas 6 for a further 30 minutes. Leave to cool before taking out of the tart ring and slicing.

WINES

Canada's crowning glory in the wine industry is Icewine. It's still made in the traditional way, using grapes that have been frozen on vine and harvested in freezing January weather. The result is nectar but with a good bite so it's not too sickly. Late harvest Riesling from down under has lemony tones that also work well with this pie, as does a Tokaji 5 Puttonyos.

ICEWINE
LATE HARVEST NEW WORLD RIESLING
AUSTRIAN TOKAJI 5 PUTTONYOS

Chocolate Chip Cookies
with Brandy-soaked Prunes

*This is indulgent and calorie-laden — but tell yourself that prunes are good
for you. You need to start this recipe by marinating the prunes a week ahead.*

SERVES 6
110g butter
80g soft dark brown sugar
80g caster sugar
1 whole egg
1 tsp vanilla essence
250g plain flour, sifted
½ tsp salt
½ tsp baking powder
80g extra-bitter chocolate,
    chopped into chips
300ml crème fraîche for
    serving

Prunes
180g caster sugar
24 prunes (preferably from
    Agen), stoned
200ml brandy

Preheat the oven to 190°C/gas 5. Cream the butter with the sugars, egg
and vanilla essence. Gradually work in the sifted flour, salt and baking
powder, then quickly mix in the chocolate. Spoon onto a non-stick
baking sheet and shape into rounds. The mix should make 18 cookies.
Bake for 10 minutes and cool on a wire rack.

For the prunes Mix the sugar with 200ml of water and bring to the
boil for 3–4 minutes. Leave to cool and when tepid, add the stoned
prunes and brandy. Cover tightly and refrigerate. Leave to marinate
for at least a week – these prunes can keep for years but seldom get
the chance!

Serving Drain the prunes and reduce the marinade over high
heat until syrupy. Put the prunes back in the pan with the reduced
marinade, cover and re-heat. Place three cookies on each plate with
prunes in between and a generous spoonful of crème fraîche.

WINES
Three different but equally good choices: the nutty Malmsey for
sophistication, the Muscat de Rivesaltes for gulping or the rich
warming brandy for slow sipping and enjoyment.

MALMSEY MADEIRA
MUSCAT DE RIVESALTES
OLD SPANISH BRANDY

Chocolate Swiss Roll with Coffee Cream

Chocolate, coffee and cream...need I say more?

Preheat the oven to 200°C/gas 6. Sift the flour and cocoa powder together. Whisk the eggs and sugar until firm and pale, then fold in the flour and cocoa. Spread the mixture into a greased, lined Swiss roll tin or pastry tray, about 20 x 40cm, and bake for 12–14 minutes or until springy to touch. Make the coffee syrup by stirring the sugar into the hot coffee until melted

Dust a clean cloth with caster sugar. Turn the sponge out onto it and remove the lining paper. Brush the sponge with coffee syrup, then cover and leave to cool for 10 minutes.

Whisk the yolks, icing sugar and butter until creamed and pale. Dissolve the instant coffee in the espresso and add to the mixture with the mascarpone. Continue to whisk until smooth and light.

Spread the coffee cream evenly on the sponge, then roll up tightly from the short edge. Cover well and refrigerate for at least 2 hours before slicing and serving.

WINES

Maury and Banyuls, sweet French reds from the Pyrenées, both have notes of chocolate and coffee so work well with desserts containing these flavours. The Recioto, which is made with half-dried and shrivelled grapes, is not as sweet as the French fortified wines but just as strong.

MAURY
BANYULS
RECIOTO DELLA VALPOLICELLA

SERVES 10
120g plain flour
30g cocoa powder
5 whole eggs
140g caster sugar

Coffee syrup
1 tbsp dark muscovado
  sugar
125ml espresso or very
  strong coffee

Coffee cream
2 yolks
120g icing sugar
80g butter
1 espresso coffee
2 tbsp instant coffee
2 tbsp mascarpone

Chocolate Mousse with Oranges and Whisky

SERVES 8–10

Chocolate mousse
6 egg whites
325g caster sugar
250g butter
6 yolks
50g cocoa powder
1 tbsp finely chopped
  orange peel confit
50ml whisky
125g extra-bitter chocolate,
  melted
125g milk chocolate,
  melted

Chocolate genoise
4 eggs
125g caster sugar
25g melted butter
125g flour, sifted
25g cocoa powder

Chocolate glaze
250ml double cream
150g liquid glucose
1 tbsp vegetable oil
1 tbsp water
200g extra-bitter chocolate,
  broken up into pieces
6 oranges, peeled and
  segmented
about 60ml of Drambuie

Chocolate mousse Start by making an Italian meringue. Whisk the egg whites until stiff. Dissolve the sugar in 125ml of water and bring to the boil. Skim and continue to cook until it reaches 120°C. Gently pour the sugar mixture onto the whisked egg whites, while continuing to whisk – this is best done with a machine. Keep on whisking until the mixture is cool and very smooth. Beat the butter, egg yolks and cocoa powder until light, then mix in the orange peel, whisky and melted chocolate. Finally fold in the Italian meringue. Pour this onto the chocolate genoise that has been soaked in the liquid. from the orange garnish (see below). Smooth the surface and refrigerate for at least 2 hours before glazing, or freeze for an hour. Remove the ring from the mousse and pour over the glaze to cover completely.

Chocolate genoise Preheat the oven to 190°C/gas 5. Whisk the eggs with the sugar in a double boiler, or a bowl over a pan of simmering water, until stiff, pale and tepid. Take off the heat then fold in the melted butter, sifted flour and cocoa powder. Butter a 22cm round tin. Pour in the mixture and bake for 18 minutes or until a knife comes out clean. Take out of the tin and leave to cool on a wire rack. When cool, trim the cake and cut it in half through the middle. Freeze the other half for another time.

Chocolate glaze Mix the cream, glucose, oil and water in a pan and bring to the boil. Whisk in the chocolate and bring back to the boil.

Garnish Douse the orange segments with Drambuie and leave to marinate in the fridge for at least a 2 hours. Serve with the mousse. You can also decorate with orange crisps. Slice an orange as thinly as possible. Dust the slices with icing sugar, place between two sheets of baking parchment and put in a cool oven, 100°C/below gas 1, to dry.

WINES
SINGLE MALT 10 YEARS SPEYSIDE
ICED DRAMBUIE
TOKAJI 5 PUTTONYOS

Bitter Chocolate Cake with Kirsch-soaked Cherries

This is almost a forêt noire, but in my view better and lighter. It's more of a cake to serve in the afternoon than a dessert, although it would be a good choice if you're only serving two courses.

SERVES 10

75g plain flour

75g cocoa powder

75g ground hazelnuts

9 egg yolks

150g caster sugar

6 egg whites

1 tbsp melted butter

250g jar of Griottines (cherries soaked in Kirsch syrup)

icing sugar and extra chocolate for decoration

Mousse

400g butter

220g extra-bitter chocolate (70 per cent cocoa), broken into pieces

40g cocoa powder

6 yolks

6 egg whites

280g sugar

Preheat the oven to 200°C/gas 6. Sieve the flour, cocoa and ground hazelnuts. Whisk the yolks and sugar until pale and stiff, then fold in the dry ingredients. Whisk the egg whites until stiff, then fold into the mix with the melted butter. Pour into a buttered, lined cake tin, about 20 x 3cm. Bake for 18–20 minutes, then leave to cool in the tin. When cold, cut across in half and trim the top to make a flat, even surface.

Mousse Gently melt the butter and chocolate in a double boiler. Do not allow to overheat. Take off the heat and mix in the cocoa powder and yolks. Whisk the whites and once they are frothy, add the sugar and continue to whisk until stiff. Fold this into the chocolate.

Assembly Drain the cherries and moisten both halves of chocolate sponge with the Kirsch syrup. Spread some of the mousse over the first layer of sponge, add the cherries in an even layer and then more mousse. Place the second layer of cake on top, moisten with a little more Kirsch syrup, then cover completely with chocolate mousse. Refrigerate for at least 4 hours before cutting. Decorate with chocolate curls and dust with icing sugar.

WINES

Italian fortified wine is flavoured with wild berries and bitter cherries. It's delicious and works beautifully with this kind of dessert. A ruby port, with its straightforward fruitiness also goes well with the cherries. And for something different and very potent, try an old Kirsch served cold in small doses.

VISCIOLATA (ITALIAN FORTIFIED WINE)

RUBY PORT

VERY COLD VIEUX KIRSCH

Milk Chocolate Mousse Scented with Ginger

Milky and chocolatey with a bite of ginger, this is perfect for those who are not keen on dark, bitter chocolate. It keeps for a couple of days in the refrigerator.

Melt the chocolate gently over a double boiler. Whip the cream until stiff. Soak the gelatine in cold water until soft, then melt it in the warm rum. Whisk the gelatine mixture with the egg and ginger in a double boiler until it is pale, frothy and forms peaks. Fold in the melted chocolate and finally the whipped whipping cream. Pour into individual ramekins or a big glass bowl. Refrigerate for at least a couple of hours. Just before serving, garnish with the biscuits and confit.

Garnish biscuits Preheat the oven to 190°C/gas 5. Whisk the egg whites with the sugar and ground hazelnuts until smooth. Add the flour and butter, then leave to rest for 1 hour. Spoon heaped teaspoons of the mixture onto a non-stick baking sheet and push down slightly to make circles – the mix will spread a little. Bake for 7–8 minutes until golden brown. Take the biscuits off the tray and while still hot, curl each one round a piece of doweling or the handle of a wooden spoon into a cigar shape. Leave to cool.

Ginger confit Cut the ginger into thin julienne. Blanch 3 times in boiling water. Put in a pan with enough water to cover and add the caster sugar. Simmer until tender and translucent. Remove and cool.

WINES
Sweet reds are not appropriate with this milky chocolate, but a rich, amber Madeira, with its nutty flavour, works well. A sweet sherry with Pedro Ximenez grapes is also a good choice. And a sweet Tokaji suits the creaminess of the mousse.

MALMSEY MADEIRA
PEDRO XIMENEZ SHERRY
TOKAJI 5 PUTTONYOS

SERVES 6
150g milk chocolate,
  roughly chopped
250g whipping cream
1 leaf gelatine
40ml white rum, warmed
1 egg
½ tsp ground ginger

Garnish
4 egg whites
110g caster sugar
125g ground hazelnuts
60g flour
75g butter, melted

Ginger confit
7cm root ginger, peeled
3 tbsp caster sugar

Christmas Pudding

It is difficult to make Christmas pudding in small batches — it just doesn't seem right — so make plenty and give the extras away as presents. This recipe makes enough for two large basins but you can make whatever size you want. Only the cooking times will vary. I usually make the puddings in September and store them in a dark cool place or in the fridge until Christmas. They can, however, be kept for a year if refrigerated.

SERVES 16
(fills two 2-litre pudding
   basins)
500g raisins
300g sultanas
300g currants
190g whole blanched
   almonds
375g suet
juice and zest of 1 orange
   and 1 lemon
1 medium carrot, peeled
   and grated
1 large Bramley apple,
   peeled and grated
200g breadcrumbs (white
   bread and brioche)
375g soft light brown sugar
6 whole eggs
1 pinch salt
1 tsp cinnamon
2 tsp mixed spice
125g candied peel, chopped
125g glacé cherries
330ml Guinness
60ml brandy
200g plain flour

Put all the ingredients in a very big mixing bowl — or even the kitchen sink! Mix well, then cover and refrigerate for at least 24 hours — if you don't have space in the fridge, just leave in a cool place. Fill the pudding basins up to 2cm below the rim. Cover with greaseproof paper, then a cloth and tie tightly with string. Place in a double-boiler or steamer and cover. Bring to a simmer and cook for 1 hour, topping up with boiling water when necessary. Transfer to a bain-marie or a shallow pan filled with water and bake in the oven, 150°C/gas 2, for a further hour and half without the lid. Remove and check whether the pudding is cooked by gently pressing the top with your fingers — it should be firm to the touch. Alternatively, insert a knife into the pudding — it should come out clean. Leave to cool. Tie on a clean cloth and wipe the basin before putting away.

To serve, put the pudding back into a double boiler or steamer with a loose-fitting lid and simmer for 3 hours. Turn out on to a dish. Warm some brandy or dark rum, pour over the pudding and ignite to serve. Accompany with some double cream.

WINES
The flavours of Matusalem Sherry are so intense it is almost like drinking Christmas pudding — not a wine for glugging. Surprisingly, Port is a good match for the pudding and you can carry on drinking it with the Stilton afterwards 'à l'Anglaise'. But at home we usually have Sauternes — à la Française!

MATUSALEM SHERRY
LBV PORT
SAUTERNES

Chocolate and Pear Tart

More chocolate — this time in a tart. Serve cold and on the day it is made, otherwise the pastry will go soft.

SERVES 6
300g caster sugar
2 sticks cinnamon
3 William pears, peeled,
   cored and halved

Sweet pastry
120g butter, softened
250g plain flour
60g caster sugar
1 egg yolk
½ tbsp double cream

Chocolate filling
120ml double cream
60g butter, cut into small
   pieces
250g extra-bitter dark
   chocolate, chopped

Put the sugar and cinnamon in a pan with 400ml of water and bring to the boil. Add the peeled, cored and halved pears. Cover and simmer for 10 minutes or until the pears are tender. Leave to cool in the syrup.

Sweet pastry Mix the soft butter, flour and sugar together using your fingertips. Gradually add the yolk and cream until the pastry comes together. Do not overwork. Wrap in clingfilm and refrigerate for at least a couple of hours.

Preheat the oven to 180°C/gas 4. Butter a fluted tart tin, 22cm in diameter. Roll out the pastry on a lightly floured surface and line the mould. Cut the edges flush with the sides and prick the base with a fork. Line with greaseproof paper and dry beans, then bake for 15 minutes. Remove the paper and beans and put back in the oven until golden and fully cooked, about another 10 minutes. Leave to cool in the tin.

Chocolate filling Bring the cream to the boil. Add the chopped butter and chocolate and whisk well until completely melted.

Assembly Pour the chocolate filling into the tart. Drain the pears on a tea towel until completely dry. Slice them across, fan out and place in the tart, keeping their shape. Refrigerate for 45 minutes before taking out of the mould and attempting to cut.

WINES
Sweet reds such as Rasteau or Banyuls, the vin doux naturel of the Pyrenées, marry well with dark chocolate. For a change, and because of the pears in this recipe, try a lighter Madeira, such as Bual.

RASTEAU

BANYULS

BUAL MADEIRA

Tarte Tatin aux Pommes

An old favourite and difficult to beat, this is always extra nice with crème fraîche or vanilla ice cream. Use a copper pan for the best results. You could use a cast-iron pan instead, but it's not as good.

Roll out the pastry on a floured work surface to about 3mm thick and 26cm in diameter. Keep in a cool place or covered in the fridge for at least an hour.

Smother the bottom of a copper pan with the butter and sprinkle over the sugar. Lay the peeled, cored and halved apples, core side up, in the pan. Squeeze them in as tight as they will get. Place the pastry on top and tuck the excess pastry into the pan between the apples and side of the pan. Prick the pastry a few times with a fork to let out steam.

Preheat the oven to 200°C/gas 6. Place the pan over a moderate to high heat on top of the stove for 15–20 minutes. Using a pallet knife, lift a little of the pastry away from the sides to ensure even cooking. The butter should be bubbling and an amber caramel colour. Place the pan in the oven and cook for 20 minutes. Remove and leave to cool for at least 1 hour. Just before serving, put back on the stove for 4–5 minutes to loosen the caramel from the pan. Place a plate or dish on top and, holding the plate on top of the pan, quickly turn it over so the pastry is beneath the mass of apples and caramel. Serve at once.

WINES

Vin de Constance is a perfect match for caramelised apple, but the real traditionalists, especially those from Normandy, would go for a bottle-conditioned sweet cider with this dish. The Muscat has a good level of acidity that matches well with apple.

VIN DE CONSTANCE
BOTTLED-CONDITIONED SWEET CIDER
MUSCAT DE CAP CORSE

SERVES 4
240g puff pastry
120g butter
180g caster sugar
5 or 6 Cox apples, peeled,
    cored and halved

Warm Quince Tart with Verbena Cream

SERVES 6
1kg caster sugar
6 quince, peeled and cut
 into quarters
juice and zest of 1 lemon

Sweet pastry
2 yolks
1 tbsp double cream
300g plain flour
60g caster sugar
100g butter, softened

Verbena cream
300ml milk
50ml double cream
4 yolks
75g caster sugar
1 small bunch of fresh
 lemon verbena (if no
 fresh verbena is available
 use dried, but not
 verbena tea bags)

Mix the caster sugar with 1 litre of water and bring to the boil. Leave to cool, then add the quince, lemon juice and zest. Bring to the boil and simmer for 30 minutes. Leave the quince to cool in the syrup.

Sweet pastry Mix the yolks and cream together. Using your fingertips, bring in the flour, sugar and softened butter. Do not overwork, but knead the pastry enough to bring it together and make a ball. Wrap in clingfilm and refrigerate for at least an hour. Roll out to a thickness of 3–4mm and cut out a circle 22cm in diameter. Prick with a fork.

Verbena cream Bring the milk and cream to the boil. Whisk the yolks and sugar together until pale and creamy. Pour in the milk and cream and whisk well. Return the mixture to the pan and cook gently, stirring with a spatula until it thickens. Do not boil or you will get scrambled eggs. As soon as it has thickened, pass through a fine sieve and add the verbena. Cover, leave to infuse until cold, and strain again.

Assembly Preheat the oven to 150°C/gas 2. Lay the quince in an ovenproof pan, 20cm wide and at least 4cm high. Add 4 tablespoons of the syrup and place the pan in the oven for 40 minutes. Add a little more syrup if the caramel becomes too dark. Take out of the oven and place the circle of sweet pastry on the quince, tucking it in between the pan and fruit. Put back in the oven and raise the temperature to 200°C/gas 6 to cook the pastry. It should be golden and cooked in 15–18 minutes. Remove and leave to cool for 10 minutes. Place a plate slightly bigger than the pan on top and quickly turn the pan over to release the tart onto the serving plate. Serve with the verbena cream.

WINES
All three of these wines should have enough freshness to respond well to the fragrant quince.

AUSTRALIAN BOTRYTIS SÉMILLON
VIN DE CONSTANCE
CANADIAN ICEWINE

Poached White Peaches Scented with Rose Petals and Wild Strawberries

The heady scent of wild strawberries and rose petals is enough to tempt even the most jaded palate. This seems almost too beautiful to eat — until you try the first spoonful.

SERVES 6

8 ripe white peaches

600g caster sugar

juice of 1 lemon

2 tbsp of dry edible rose buds

or

3 tbsp of fresh untreated rose petals from highly scented flowers

or

4 tsp or more to taste of edible rosewater available from healthfood shops or chemists

5 leaves gelatine, softened in cold water

rose petals for decoration

400g wild strawberries

icing sugar

Blanch the peaches in boiling water for 15 seconds. Plunge them into iced water, drain and peel. Mix the sugar and lemon juice in a large pan with 600ml of water and bring to the boil. Add the peeled peaches, cover and simmer for 10–15 minutes until tender, turning the peaches around occasionally. Add the rose flavouring and leave to cool.

Take 100ml of the syrup and bring back to the boil. Add the gelatine that has been softened in cold water and squeezed dry. Whisk until the gelatine has completely melted, then add a further 400ml of the syrup. Cool again.

Cut the peaches into 8 slices each and arrange in bowls, plates or glasses. Cover with the cold, but not yet set syrup, and decorate with rose petals, wild strawberries and a dusting of icing sugar.

WINES

A good Moscato d'Asti is light and fizzy, with slightly sweet, flowery notes. It can be difficult to find, but is well worth the trouble. Less scented but equally good with wild strawberries is the Champagne demi-sec. Prosecco is the bubbly that should be used for the classic Bellini – a cocktail of sparkling wine and peach nectar – so the obvious choice to serve with peaches.

MOSCATO D'ASTI

CHAMPAGNE DEMI-SEC

PROSECCO

Upside-down Pineapple Cake

This is an incredibly light cake, delicious at any time of day.

SERVES 6

1 medium-size golden
  pineapple
2 tbsp butter
100g plus 1 tbsp caster
  sugar
2 eggs
2 tbsp crème fraîche
4 tbsp vegetable oil
160g plain flour
50g ground almonds
1 tsp heaped baking powder
2 tsp ground cinnamon

Top and tail the pineapple, then trim down the sides and remove the eyes. Cut into 1cm slices and remove the core. Butter a 20cm cake tin, taking extra care with the base, and sprinkle with a tablespoon of caster sugar. Arrange the pineapple slices on top of the sugar.

Preheat the oven to 180°C/gas 4. Whisk the eggs, crème fraîche and oil with the rest of the sugar until light and fluffy. Mix in the flour, ground almonds, baking powder and cinnamon and beat until smooth. Pour this batter over the pineapple slices and bake for 35–40 minutes. Leave to cool a little before turning out. Serve warm with crème fraîche.

WINES

Many Sauternes have a hint of pineapple, so this wine is a good match for the cake. Lunel is a beautiful village in the Gard region that produces some very exciting sweet muscats with a really fruity base. You could also try an Eiswein from Germany, made from late-harvest frozen grapes. Most of the liquid is removed as ice which concentrates the sweetness and flavour. Most Eisweins are well balanced and have a low alcohol content.

SAUTERNES
MUSCAT DE LUNEL
EISWEIN

French Toast with Vanilla Cream and Golden Sultanas

I use brioche bread for this recipe, as it is richer than plain bread. It also has a great depth of flavour. You can make your own brioche or buy it at a good bakery. This dessert can also be made with panettone or pandoro.

Place the sultanas in a pan with the split vanilla pods, taking care to scrape out the seeds to extract the maximum taste. Add the wine, 3 tablespoons of the sugar and 100ml of water. Simmer for 10 minutes, stirring to melt the sugar and plump the sultanas, then leave to cool.

Whisk the whipping cream until it forms peaks and add the crème fraîche. Add a little of the cold syrup from the sultanas and the vanilla essence.

Whisk the single cream, egg and the remaining tablespoon of caster sugar together. Dip the slices of brioche into this mixture, leaving them just long enough to soften, a matter of seconds. Heat the butter in a frying pan. When it is foaming, add the soaked brioche and cook gently on both sides to crisp and brown. Drizzle with the vanilla syrup and dust with a little icing sugar and cinnamon. Serve immediately with the sultanas and vanilla cream.

WINES
Bugey is a region just northeast of Lyon, which occasionally produces a wine made with grapes dried on hay. This wine is probably not as fashionable as the other sweet wines, but well worth finding. It matches the sultanas in flavour.

VIN DE PAILLE FROM BUGEY

VIN DE CONSTANCE

AUSTRALIAN BOTRYTIS SÉMILLON

SERVES 4

140g golden sultanas
2 vanilla pods, split
125ml sweet white wine
  (Tokaji, Sauternes etc)
4 tbsp caster sugar
200ml whipping cream
2 tbsp crème fraîche
1 tsp vanilla essence
6 tbsp single cream
1 whole egg
brioche, cut into 8 slices
  1cm thick and about 6cm
  across and crusts
  removed
2 tbsp butter
icing sugar
ground cinnamon

Warm Olive Oil Cake with Lavender and Roasted Figs

This is Provence on a plate. Be sure to choose purple figs from September's harvest, when they are at their sweetest and best.

SERVES 6

2 eggs

80g light brown sugar

80ml olive oil

30ml sweet Madeira

1 heaped tsp lavender flowers

125g plain flour

½ tsp baking powder

10–12 figs, purple variety from September crop

80g butter, plus extra for greasing the moulds

4 tbsp clear honey, preferably lavender scented

juice of 2 lemons

Preheat the oven to 180°C/gas 4. Butter 6 little flan moulds, 5 x 2cm in size. Whisk the eggs and sugar until frothy. Add the olive oil, Madeira and lavender and continue whisking. Finally fold in the flour and baking powder. Pour into the moulds and bake for 12–15 minutes until golden and firm to the touch.

Turn the oven up to 220°C/gas 7. Cut a cross in each fig from the tip to halfway down. Open the figs up slightly and place a knob of butter in each. Put the figs in a roasting pan, drizzle with honey and bake for 6–8 minutes. Remove the figs and put them on top of the warm cakes. Put the roasting pan on the stove and pour in the lemon juice. Bring to the boil, stir and spoon the juices over the figs before serving.

WINES

The Riesling goes well with the honey and lavender, as does the Muscat. The Massandra is a rare and very expensive wine from Ukraine. It can be aged for ever and if you ever get the chance to taste it you will never forget the experience.

LATE HARVEST RIESLING

ORANGE MUSCAT

MASSANDRA

Chocolate Pecan Fudge

These little fudge morsels can be served like chocolates or petits fours, perfect to serve after dinner instead of dessert. They keep for weeks in an airtight container and are extremely moreish.

MAKES ABOUT 40 PIECES
1 tbsp golden syrup
180ml milk
1 pinch of salt
500g caster sugar
90g extra-bitter chocolate,
    chopped
200g pecan nuts, roughly
    chopped
vanilla essence

Put the syrup, milk, salt, sugar and chopped chocolate in a stainless steel pan. Bring to the boil, stirring with a spatula. Put in a sugar thermometer and cook to 115°C, then take off the heat. Continue to stir until the mixture has stopped bubbling.

Add the nuts and vanilla essence and stir until the fudge goes matt and starts to emulsify. Pour into a buttered tin 28 x 20cm. Press the fudge down and even out the top. When it's cold, turn out and cut into small slices.

WINES

Coffee is a perfect partner for chocolate, and an old malt whisky is equally good. There are coffee overtones in Banyuls, too, so it suits these sweet treats.

ESPRESSO COFFEE
OLD MALT WHISKY
BANYULS

Cannelés Bordelais

These little cakes are a speciality of Bordeaux. They come in different degrees of 'doneness', light golden, golden and dark golden-brown — the darker the colour, the deeper the flavour. All should be soft and creamy in the middle and slightly crisp and chewy on the outside. Traditionally, they are made in copper moulds that are in the shape of a chef's hat and must be greased with a mixture of beeswax and butter to avoid the mixture sticking. Beeswax can be bought from some healthfood shops otherwise a trip to Bordeaux will be necessary. The moulds are also available in porcelain.

Put the vanilla pods and seeds in a pan with the milk powder, butter and 800ml of water. Whisk well and bring to the boil, then take off the heat immediately. Whisk the remaining ingredients together without overworking. Add this to the first mixture and pass through a coarse sieve. Refrigerate for 24 hours. Preheat the oven to 170°C/gas 3. Grease the moulds, stir the mixture and pour it into the moulds to just under the brim. Bake for about 40 minutes. Remove and cool for 20 minutes, then take the little cakes out of the moulds and stand them up on a baking tray. Put them back in the oven at 180°C/gas 4 until they are as golden as you wish.

WINES
As petits fours, these go with more or less anything, but they are particularly well matched by the local sweet wines, such as Barsac or Jurançon Mouelleux.

BARSAC
JURANÇON

MAKES 36 SMALL OR
12 BIG CANNELÉS
6 vanilla pods, split and
  seeds scraped out
80g milk powder
80g butter
460g Nestlé's condensed
  milk (sweetened)
580g caster sugar
320g plain flour
100ml dark rum
4 eggs
3 yolks

Red Wine Pear Tart

The striking colours make this a very beautiful tart. It needs to be eaten as soon as it is made or else the base will go soggy.

SERVES 6

7 pears (William, Guyot or
  Passe-Crassane)
500ml strong red wine
140g caster sugar
2 cinnamon sticks
juice and grated zest of
  1 lemon
450g sweet pastry (see
  page 154)

Pastry cream
4 egg yolks
60g caster sugar
25g plain flour
250ml milk
icing sugar for sprinkling
  on the top

Peel the pears, cut in quarters lengthways and remove the core. Place the pears in a pan with the wine, sugar, cinnamon, grated lemon zest and juice. Bring to a gentle simmer, cover with greaseproof paper and cook for 35 minutes. The pears should be tender. Leave them to cool, then remove and set aside. Remove the cinnamon sticks, bring the red wine mixture to the boil and reduce until syrupy.

Line a buttered tart tin, about 24cm in diameter, with the sweet pastry. Prick the base with a fork, cover with a greaseproof paper and fill with dry beans. Bake at 200°C/gas 6 for 20 minutes. Remove the beans and paper, put the pastry case back in the oven and continue to cook until golden brown. Leave to cool. Once the pastry is cool, spoon in the pastry cream to cover the base. Slice the pears and arrange on the cream. Glaze with the red wine syrup and serve.

Pastry cream Whisk the yolks and sugar until pale and add the flour. Bring the milk to the boil and pour into the eggs and sugar. Whisk this rigorously, then return to the pan. Bring back to the boil and cook, stirring continuously for 2 minutes. Once boiled, pour out of the pan into a clean bowl and sprinkle with icing sugar to avoid a crust.

WINES

Find a Rivesaltes with Hors d'Age on the label — meaning it has been aged longer than usual — to experience the full fruity, chocolatey depth that this sun-drenched wine can have. Equally rich is the Muscat from Corsica, which is a lot less tannic. Provided the pears have taken on a good red wine taste and colour, a Cape Vintage, as it is now called, or a 'port-style' wine from the Cape is also very good.

HORS D'AGE RIVESALTES
MUSCAT DE CAP CORSE
SOUTH AFRICAN PORT

Classic Raspberry Tart

When raspberries are in season and bursting with sweetness and flavour, there is no other fruit to equal them. This particular tart reminds me of my apprenticeship as a pastry chef. We would make these tarts for only eight weeks of the year.

Make a syrup by mixing the caster sugar with 125ml of water. Bring to the boil, then set aside to cool. Add the raspberry alcohol once the syrup is cool.

Preheat the oven to 200°C/gas 6. Roll out the sweet pastry on a floured surface to 2–3mm thickness and line a lightly buttered 24cm tart ring or 8 individual 8cm rings set on a baking sheet. Spoon in the almond cream until the tart is two-thirds full, then bake at 20–30 minutes until golden and fully cooked. Leave to cool, then remove the tart ring. Brush the tart with the flavoured syrup. Neatly arrange the raspberries on the tart and dust with icing sugar. Do not refrigerate. Serve with double cream and raspberry coulis.

Almond cream Beat the butter, then add the sugar and ground almonds. Continue to beat until the mixture is pale and creamy, then add the eggs one at a time.

Coulis Blitz the raspberries and sugar together – the amount of sugar depends on the ripeness of the fruit so taste before adding the full amount. Add a few drops of water if too thick.

WINES
The classic combination of Sauternes and perfectly ripe raspberries makes you go 'aahhh'! Alternatively, try an old Jurançon Moelleux or an old Beerenauslese to complement one of my all-time favourite desserts.

SAUTERNES
JURANÇON MOELLEUX
BEERENAUSLESE

SERVES 8
125g caster sugar
1 tbsp raspberry alcohol
 (40 per cent proof)
600g sweet pastry, made
 with 180g butter,
 375g flour, 90g sugar,
 2 egg yolks and 1 tbsp
 double cream (see page
 152 for method)
750g large plump
 raspberries
icing sugar

Almond cream
100g butter softened
100g icing sugar
100g ground almonds
2 eggs

Coulis
300g raspberries
60–80g icing sugar

Rich Almond and Butter Cake with Raspberries and Clotted Cream

These little cakes are best served warm, but can be made in advance, stored in an airtight container and re-heated. Clotted cream is unique and makes the French quite envious.

SERVES 6

10 egg whites
300g caster sugar
300g butter
100g plain flour
160g ground almonds
2 drops of almond essence
50g flaked almonds
600g raspberries
6 tbsp clotted cream

Blackberry syrup
250g blackberries
4 tbsp caster sugar
juice of 1 lemon

Preheat the oven to 200°C/gas 6. Whisk the egg whites and sugar together just enough to mix. Heat the butter until foaming and golden, then leave to cool. Fold the flour and ground almonds into the egg whites. Add the almond essence and butter, making sure to put in all the brown specks of the butter as well. Butter 6 individual round tins of about 6 x 1.5cm – muffin tins should be fine. Pour in the mixture and sprinkle over the flaked almonds. Bake for 10 minutes, or until puffed up and golden brown.

Serve the cakes warm with perfectly ripe raspberries, a spoonful of clotted cream and a drizzle of blackberry syrup.

Blackberry syrup Put the blackberries in a stainless steel or glass bowl and add the sugar and lemon juice. Lightly mash the berries with a fork, then cover with clingfilm and place over a pan of simmering water for 25 minutes. Leave to cool, then pass the mixture through a muslin cloth to collect the syrup.

WINES

Any excuse for a bit of fizz! It makes a refreshing change from sweet wine and this is not a very sweet dessert. I find that Barsac always goes well with cakes and the thick golden muscat from Frontignan suits those who want the sugar hit.

CHAMPAGNE ROSÉ
BARSAC
MUSCAT DE FRONTIGNAN

Orange Salad with Orange Flower Water and Olive Oil

This may sound peculiar but I assure you it works a treat. Choose an olive oil that is dark, viscous and full of rich aromas.

SERVES 4

4 oranges
4 blood oranges
2 tbsp of orange-blossom
   honey
1 tsp of orange flower
   water
2 tbsp pistachios
olive oil

With a sharp, thin-bladed knife peel the oranges and divide into segments. Squeeze the remaining cores and membranes to extract any juice. Gently fold in the honey and orange flower water, cover and refrigerate for at least an hour. Arrange the orange segments in glass bowls or soup plates with the juice, then drizzle a little olive oil on top. Sprinkle with pistachios and serve.

WINES

White Pineau is the fortified wine from the Cognac region, strong, yet soft on the palate. The degree of sweetness in Tokaji is measured in degrees of puttonyos, which is the amount of residual sugar per barrel. Three is sweet, five is very sweet, above that is sticky but delicious. Iced Cointreau is an unusual choice, but works.

PINEAU DES CHARENTES WHITE
TOKAJI 3 PUTTONYOS
ICED COINTREAU

Warm Apricot Compote with Crunchy Oatcakes

You can break open apricot stones and eat the kernels, which have an intense almond flavour. Don't eat too many, though, as they can give you indigestion!

Bring the sugar to the boil with 400ml of water to make a syrup. Add the apricots to the boiling syrup, cover and simmer for 10 minutes. Gently stir and leave to cool. The apricots should be soft but still retain some of their shape.

Oatcakes Melt the sugar, honey and butter together in a pan. Stir in the oats and 2 tablespoons of almonds. Place 4 non-stick rings, about 8cm x 2cm, on a baking sheet. Put some mixture into each ring and press down well. Refrigerate until set. To serve, take the oatcakes out of the rings, place on a non-stick baking mat and bake in a warm oven at 170°C/gas 3 for 4–5 minutes until just tepid. Remove with a palette knife and arrange on plates with the drained apricots on top. Drizzle the caramel sauce round them and add a sprinkling of toasted sliced almonds.

Caramel sauce Mix the sugars and butter in a pan and cook until bubbling and caramelised, stirring nearly all the time. Pour in the cream while continuing to stir. You may need to pass this through a fine sieve.

WINES

Sauternes is a versatile wine and has an affinity with poached fruits such as apricots. If you want something with more of a floral note, the Alsace is not too sweet and immensely fragrant. The unusual white wine of Madiran comes also as a moelleux and is very good if aged in oak.

MUSCAT D'ALSACE SÉLECTION DE GRAINS NOBLES
SAUTERNES
PACHERENC DU VIC BILH MOELLEUX

SERVES 4
200g caster sugar
800g large ripe apricots, cut in half and stones removed

Oatcakes
1 tbsp dark muscovado sugar
1 tbsp clear orange-blossom honey
80g butter
80g porridge oats
4 tbsp flaked almonds

Caramel sauce
1 tbsp dark muscovado
1 tbsp caster sugar
1 tbsp butter
125ml single cream

Panna Cotta with Wild Strawberries and Mango Coulis

Panna cotta literally means cooked cream and is considered Italy's comfort food. This dessert comes from the Piedmont region in Italy and originated in the mid 1800s.

SERVES 8

3 leaves gelatine

2 tbsp dark rum

600ml single cream

2 vanilla pods, split and
    seeds scraped out

100g caster sugar

peel of 1 orange, no pith

500g wild strawberries

Mango coulis

2 large ripe mangoes

2 tbsp caster sugar

juice of 1 lime

Soften the gelatine in the rum. Quickly bring the cream, vanilla pods and seeds, sugar and orange peel to simmering point, stirring to avoid it catching. Immediately take off the heat and stir in the gelatine and rum. Leave to cool, then remove the vanilla pods, and orange peel.

Pour the mixture into moulds or ramekins measuring about 5cm across and 4cm high or taller. Put them in the refrigerator and leave for at least 8 hours to set. To turn out the panna cottas, place the in very hot water for 5–6 seconds. Run a knife around the edge and gently coax out on to a plate. Arrange the strawberries and mango coulis decoratively around each panna cotta.

Mango coulis Peel the mangoes and remove the stones. Place the mango flesh in a blender with the sugar and lime juice. Blitz until smooth and pass through a fine sieve. If the mango is not very juicy you may need to add a tablespoon or two of water.

WINES

This delicate dessert needs a sensitive, seductive wine. The two Italian suggestions will certainly fit the bill, but if you want to go French, look no further than a silky, sweet Vouvray.

MOSCATO D'ASTI

RECIOTO DI SOAVE

OLD VOUVRAY MOELLEUX

Coupe of Fruit and Berries Scented with Herbs

The combination of fruits is up to you. Choose whatever fruit you like that is ripe and in season. Serve on a hot summer day in glass bowls or in old-fashioned champagne glasses.

SERVES 6

100g golden caster sugar
200ml sweet white wine
juice of 1 lemon
750g of assorted berries,
   wild strawberries,
   strawberries, raspberries,
   blueberries, blackberries,
   red currants, cherries
1 mango
2 kiwi fruits
1 sprig each of mint,
   coriander and basil,
   roughly chopped

To make the syrup, bring the sugar, wine and lemon juice to the boil. Stir well and leave to cool.

Wash and pick over all the berries, hull the strawberries and slice if necessary. Cut the cherries in half and remove the stones. Peel and dice the mango and kiwi. Place all the fruit in a large bowl and douse with the syrup. Chill for an hour and gently toss a couple of times. Add the coarsely chopped herbs to taste.

Divide between the bowls or champagne glasses. As you are just about to tuck in, add a splash of Champagne or sparkling wine to each serving to give a little fizz and freshness.

WINES

The Clairette sparkling semi-sweet wine, scented with Muscat grape, has to be tasted. It's very underrated. Crémant is lightly sparkling. The Limoux version is fragrant if not quite as sweet as the Clairette.

CLAIRETTE DE DIE
CRÉMANT DE LIMOUX
MOSCATI

Sponge Biscuits with Fruit Compotes

Make two or three compotes to serve together and experiment with different flavours and spices. You could even add a little pepper or chilli to some.

SERVES 6

Apricot compote
10 large apricots, stoned
  and halved
2–3 tbsp caster sugar

Strawberry compote
500g strawberries, washed,
  hulled and cut in half
4 tbsp caster sugar
1 tbsp lemon juice

Peach and vanilla
4 white peaches
2 tbsp caster sugar
100ml sweet white wine
1 vanilla pod, split

Blackberry and thyme
300g blackberries, washed
3 tbsp dark muscovado
  sugar
2 sprigs of thyme

Sponge biscuits
6 eggs, separated
190g caster sugar
180g plain flour
icing sugar for dusting

Apricot compote Place the apricots in a pan and add the sugar and 3 tablespoons of water. Cover and gently simmer for 10 minutes, stirring occasionally.

Strawberry compote Place the strawberries in a pan with the sugar, lemon juice and 4 tablespoons of water. Cover and simmer until soft.

Peach and vanilla Blanch the peaches in boiling water for 10 seconds. Refresh in iced water and remove the skins. Cut in halves and discard the stones. Place in pan with the sugar, wine and vanilla pod, cover and simmer until soft.

Blackberry and thyme Place the blackberries in a pan with the sugar, thyme and 4 tablespoons of water. Cover and simmer for 10 minutes or until soft, stirring occasionally.

Sponge biscuits Preheat the oven to 220°C/gas 7. Whisk the egg yolks with two-thirds of the sugar until the mixture is pale, with a ribbon consistency. In a clean bowl whisk the egg whites until risen, add the remaining sugar and continue to whisk until firm. Fold about one-third of the whites into the yolk mixture with a slotted spoon. When fully mixed, add the rest of the whites and gently fold in. When the whites are almost incorporated, add the flour and gently mix in. Keep the mixture very light and airy and don't over-mix. Pipe strips of the mixture, 10cm x 2cm, on to a baking mat, dust with icing sugar and bake in the hot oven for 8 minutes. Leave to cool a little before lifting onto a wire rack.

WINES
Stay with the classic combination of slightly sweet bubbles with biscuits. It always works.

MOSCATO D'ASTI
CHAMPAGNE DEMI-SEC

Salted Caramel Walnut Tart

If possible, use fresh walnuts from the Périgord region in October and November. It's worth the extra effort of cracking them open yourself.

Roll out the paste to line a flan ring measuring about 22cm across by 3cm high. Keep back about a third of the paste to make the lattice top.

Preheat the oven to 180°C/gas 4. Bring the single cream and butter to the boil and set aside. In a deep, thick-bottomed pan, mix the glucose and sugar with 100ml of water and place over high heat. Stir well with a spatula and cook until a rich brown caramel colour. Reduce the heat, then slowly pour in the cream and butter, stirring well all the time. Finally add the walnuts and take off the heat.

When the filling is cool, pour into the lined flan ring. Decorate with a lattice of strips cut with the remaining paste. Bake in the preheated oven for 30 minutes. Leave to cool before removing the ring.

WINES

Amaretto works well with the salty-sweet tastes and the nuts. A red Muscat liqueur from Australia is sweet enough to equal this sticky treat or you could choose a Tawny Port   port and walnuts are a classic combination.

AMARETTO
AUSTRALIAN MUSCAT LIQUEUR
TAWNY PORT

SERVES 10
600g sweet pastry made
  with 450g flour, 150g
  butter, 90g sugar, 4 egg
  yolks and 2 tbsp cream
  (see page 154 for method)
100ml single cream
200g salted butter
200g glucose
400g caster sugar
400g walnuts, shelled
  weight

Apricot and Coconut Spring Roll with Grilled Chilli Pineapple

Fresh coconut is a must for this recipe — the desiccated stuff just isn't the same. Don't leave out the chilli as it gives a wonderful kick.

SERVES 4

1 small sweet pineapple
250g caster sugar
2 cinnamon sticks
2 red chillies, medium heat,
   cut in half
20 dried apricots
1 tbsp cornflour
125ml coconut cream
1 fresh coconut, flesh
   removed and grated
12 sheets of brique pastry
   (North African paper-
   thin pancakes) or spring
   roll pastry
vegetable oil for deep frying

Peel the pineapple and cut into 4 slices. Remove the core with a round cutter. Make a syrup with the sugar, cinnamon, chillies and 400ml of water. Once boiled, add the pineapple and dried apricots, simmer for 3 minutes, then leave to cool.

Moisten the cornflour with 1 tablespoon of the syrup. Heat up the coconut cream, bring to a simmer and whisk in the cornflour. Bring back to a simmer, then take off the heat. Add the grated coconut and leave to cool. Remove the apricots and pineapple from the syrup. Chop the apricots and add to the coconut mix.

To make the chilli syrup, slice one of the chillies, add to 8 table-spoons of syrup and set aside.

Square off the sheets of pastry and discard the trimmings. Divide the apricot and coconut mixture between the sheets, placing some in the middle of each one. Neatly roll up each parcel, tucking in the edges and sealing them with a little water. Heat the oil in a deep fryer or large pan. Deep fry the rolls until crispy. Serve hot with the slices of pineapple, grilled on a griddle to reheat and mark, and drizzle with chilli syrup. Decorate with cinnamon sticks.

WINES

A dark rum would suit the tropical spirit of this dish. For something of a change, a Gewürztraminer, with its spicy lychee notes, goes well. And for a classic sweet wine, the golden Muscat from the Greek island of Samos will not disappoint.

OLD DARK RUM
GEWÜRZTRAMINER
SAMOS

Passion Fruit Soufflé

This is a permanent fixture at Le Gavroche and a best seller.
It's tangy and sweet, light but wicked.

SERVES 6
24 passion fruits, plus 6
    extra for decoration
juice of 1 orange
2 tbsp cornflour
8 egg whites
280g caster sugar, plus extra
    for dusting the moulds
6 vanilla macaroons
icing sugar for dusting

Cut the 24 passion fruits in half and scoop out the flesh and seeds. Put in a blender with the orange juice and blitz for a few seconds, just enough to break up the passion fruit flesh and fibres. Do not over-process or the pips will break up. Press the mixture though a fine sieve and discard the pips. Put in a pan and boil until reduced by half. Dissolve the cornflour in a tiny amount of water, then whisk into the boiling passion fruit mixture to thicken. Take off the heat and leave to cool.

Preheat the oven to 200°C/gas 6. Butter 6 soufflé moulds (7cm across by 6cm deep) and dust with caster sugar. Whisk the egg whites until frothy and gradually add the sugar. Continue to whisk until firm. Mix one-third of the egg whites with the passion fruit mixture, then gently fold in the rest. Half fill the moulds and place a macaroon in each. Fill to the top with passion fruit mixture and smooth over the tops with a palette knife. Run the point of a knife round the edge of each dish to help the soufflé rise straight. Put in the preheated oven for 7–8 minutes.

Dust the soufflés with icing sugar. Scoop out the remaining passion fruits to place on top of each soufflé. For even more of a treat, serve with white chocolate ice cream.

WINES
The flowery sweetness of Muscat and Moscatel marry well with the passion fruit, but a Sauternes is my first choice. Château Gilette Crème de Tête is sublime – its peculiarity is that the wine is stored in concrete vats.

ALSACE MUSCAT SÉLECTION DE GRAINS NOBLES
ALICANTE MOSCATEL
SAUTERNES

Pistachio and Honey Baklava

These delicious little treats are best served as petits fours or an afternoon treat — crispy, sweet and just a little naughty.

Preheat the oven to 180°C/gas 4. Gently melt the butter and honey in a pan. Stir in the spices, vanilla essence and very finely grated lemon zest. Butter a non-stick buttered rectangular tin, about 26cm wide and 6 cm deep. Lay a base of 3 sheets of filo, brushing each sheet generously with the butter and honey mix. Mix together the chopped pistachios and ground almonds. Sprinkle a third of them over the filo. Repeat these layers twice more and finish with 3 sheets of filo. Bake in the oven for 20–25 minutes until golden.

Meanwhile, boil 125ml of water with the lemon juice and caster sugar. Add the orange flower water and pour while still warm over the baklava. Cover with greaseproof paper and a light weight to press everything down slightly, then leave to cool for an hour or so. Turn out and cut into small cubes.

WINES
Sweet mint tea, North African-style, is perfect, but an intense Muscat from South Africa or a Rhine Botrytis Riesling will also be heavenly.

SWEET MINT TEA
SOUTH AFRICAN MUSCAT
TROCKENBEERENAUSLESE

SERVES 8

250g butter
6 tbsp clear honey
1 tsp cinnamon powder
a pinch of cloves
2 tsp vanilla essence
zest of 1 lemon
12 sheets of filo pastry
600g peeled unsalted
  pistachios, coarsely
  chopped
60g ground almonds
juice of lemon
300g caster sugar
2 tsp edible orange
  flower water

Fine Wines
Usually you choose a wine to go with the food you are serving, but sometimes when you have a special bottle you will want to plan the menu around it. Here are some suggestions for very fine wines and dishes to complement them.

HOPLER TROCKENBEERENAUSLESE 1999

Simply the best example of Austrian noble rot, this grand sticky wine from the region of Burgenland is a serious a tipple as they come. 'Beeren' means berries and 'Auslese' translates as 'out picked'. This means that the grapes are selected and picked out from particularly ripe bunches to make these rich and luscious wines. Trockenbeerenauslese means the same as above, but the grapes are dried (trocken) until almost raisin-like. This produces the most expensive, intense floral wines

Rice Pudding with Banana and Spice

SERVES 6
1 litre milk
75g caster sugar
1 vanilla pod, split
2 cloves
2 sticks cinnamon
3 cardamom pods
½ tsp ground nutmeg
200g pudding rice
4 bananas, peeled and cut
  into wedges
1 tbsp butter
1 tbsp light muscovado
  sugar
2 tbsp dark rum
1 200ml can of sweetened
  condensed milk

Banana crisps
1 under-ripe banana
icing sugar for dusting

Bring the milk to the boil with the caster sugar, split vanilla pod, cloves, cinnamon, cardamom and a little nutmeg. Sprinkle in the rice and stir. Simmer for 30 minutes, stirring occasionally to avoid sticking. Cover and leave to stand for at least 20 minutes.

Pan fry the bananas with the butter and sugar. When lightly caramelised but still firm, pour in the rum and take off the heat. Fold the condensed milk into the rice. Serve the pudding in bowls with the banana on top. Decorate with banana crisps.

Banana crisps Peel an under-ripe banana and slice it as thinly as possible lengthways. Put the slices on a non-stick baking mat, dust with icing sugar and dry out in a low oven, 110°C/gas ½, until brown and crisp. These crisps can be kept in an airtight container for a couple of days.

SCHLOSS REINHARTSHAUSEN RHEINGAU 1990 RIESLING AUSLESE

Originally the property of the Prussian royal family, a fact that is still proudly displayed on the label, this wine is refreshingly light in alcohol but high on aroma. The humidity and mist in the Rhine Valley make it one of the world's best areas for botrytis.

Lemon Syllabub with Sponge Biscuits

Wash the lemons and finely grate the skin, being careful not to take any of the bitter pith. Squeeze the juice and set aside. Put the wine in a pan with the sugar and lemon zest. Boil until reduced by half, then add the lemon juice and leave to cool completely.

Whisk the cream until it forms peaks, then slowly incorporate the lemon syrup and finally the Limoncello. Pour into chilled glasses and refrigerate for at least 2 hours before serving with some sponge biscuits.

Sponge biscuits Preheat the oven to 220°C/gas 7. Whisk the egg yolks with half the sugar until frothy and pale, then fold in the sieved flour. In a clean bowl, whisk the egg whites until they have a ribbon consistency. Add the remaining sugar and continue to whisk until firm. Gently fold this into the remaining mixture. Do not overwork. Put the mixture into a piping bag with a plain 15mm nozzle. Pipe long fingers, about 8 x 3cm, on to a non-stick sheet or baking mat. Dust with icing sugar and bake for about 8 minutes. Dust again and place on a wire rack to cool. These are best eaten day they are made.

SERVES 6
2 lemons
300ml sweet white wine
60g caster sugar
400ml double cream
4 tbsp Limoncello

Sponge biscuits
3 eggs, separated
90g caster sugar
80g plain flour
icing sugar for dusting

Wine directory

The suggestions and tips in this book are ways of enjoying both the food and the wine and have worked for me. Some are classic combinations, others not so. Wines are always changing and different vintages can sometimes change a wine so much that it may no longer work with a particular dish. However, the style is what you should look for, and remember – choosing wine is not about laying down rules, it's about enjoying yourself.

This directory is by no means a complete list of all the wines that I recommend or that you should rush out and buy! But they are particularly good examples of my recommendations. In some instances there is more than one example, but the style of the wine will be similar. The purpose of this directory is to help you to make the right choices and find wines you enjoy.

There may be times when you cannot find the exact wine I suggest, in which case look at the notes at the foot of the recipe for guidance. I have generally not specified vintages since this can be confusing and quite daunting when starting out.

As with anything to do with taste, this whole subject is open to much debate. One thing is for sure, though – the pleasure derived from tasting and experimenting with food and wine is never ending.

Château Lafite 1887
Recognised as one of the very best and most consistent of Bordeaux Grand Cru wines, Château Lafite has been made since the 17th century. It is still owned by the Rothschild family, who bought the vineyard in 1868.

Wine directory

SPARKLING WINES

FRANCE
Champagne
Bruno Paillard, Blanc de Blancs, Brut
Henriot, Blanc de Blancs
Krug Grande Cuvée
Laurent Perrier, Ultra Brut
Lenoble, Grand Cru Blanc de Blancs
P. Louis Martin, Cuvée Vincent,
  Bouzy Grand Cru
R de Ruinart, Brut
Taittinger Brut Réserve
Taittinger Demi-Sec
Veuve Cliquot Ponsardin Rich
  Réserve

Champagne Rosé
Billecart Salmon Brut
Gosset Célébris
P. Louis Martin, Bouzy Grand Cru

Cerdon Du Bugey
Montagnieu

Clairette De Die
Alchard-Vincent Demi-Sec

Crémant De Bourgogne
Kriter Patriarche

Crémant De Limoux (Blanquette)
Domaine de Fourn

Saumur Mousseux
Bouvet-Ladubay Vintage Brut Loire

AUSTRALIA
Domaine Chandon, Yarra Valley
Jansz, Tasmania
Yellowglen Vintage Brut,
  Beringer-Blass

ENGLAND
Chapel Down Rosé, Kent
Nyetimber, West Sussex

ITALY
Moscato d'Asti, Rivetti, Piedmont
Prosecco, Bisol, Veneto

NEW ZEALAND
Pelorus, Marlborough

SOUTH AFRICA
Graham Beck Winery, Robertson
Nederburg, Paarl

SPAIN
Cava Codorniu, San Sadurni de
  Noya

USA
Schramsberg Blanc de Noir, Napa

WHITE WINES

FRANCE
Alsace
 Gewürztraminer, Cuvée Tradition,
  Hugel
Gewürztraminer, Clos Windsbuhl,
  Domaine Zind Humbrecht
Gewürztraminer, Léon Beyer
Riesling Cuvée des Comtes
  d'Eguisheim, Léon Beyer
Riesling Cuvée des Ecaillers, Léon
  Beyer
Riesling Grand Cru Altenberg
  de Bergheim, Gustave Lorentz
Riesling, Clos St Hune,
  F. E. Trimbach
Riesling, Hugel
Tokay Pinot Gris, Tradition Hugel

Bordeaux
Blanc de Lynch Bages
Château Haut-Brion
Château Laville Haut-Brion
Château Pâpe Clément
Tour de Miranbeau, Entre Deux
  Mers
"Y"Lur Saluces

Burgundy
Beaune, Clos des Mouches, Joseph
  Drouhin
Bourgogne Aligoté, Louis Latour
Chablis Grand Cru Les Blanchots
  Réserve de l'Obédiencerie,
  Domaine Laroche
Chablis Grand Cru Les Clos, Fèvre
Chablis St Martin, Domaine Laroche
Corton Charlemagne, Domaine
  Bonneau du Martray
Corton Charlemagne, Domaine
  Chevalier
Mâcon Uchizy, Paul Talmard
Meursault, Clos de la Barre,
  Domaine des Comtes Lafon
Meursault, Domaine Coche Dury
Montrachet, Marquis de Laguiche,
  Joseph Drouhin
Bâtard Montrachet, Domaine Jean-
  Noël Gagnard
Chassagne Montrachet 1er Cru,
  Morgeot, Domaine Jean-Noël
  Gagnard
Chevalier Montrachet, Domaine
  Leflaive
Pouilly Fuissé, Vieilles Vignes
  Château Fuissé, M Vincent et Fils
Puligny Montrachet, 1er Cru,
  Champ Canet, Etienne Sauzet
Saint Veran, Georges Duboeuf

Côtes du Rhône
Châteauneuf du Pâpe, Domaine de
  la Janasse
Châteauneuf du Pâpe, Clos des
  Papes, Paul Avril
Condrieu (Viognier), Les Chaillet,
  Yves Cuilleron
Costières de Nîmes, Mas Neuf,
  Viognier de Nîmes
Crozes Hermitage, Chapoutier
Crozes Hermitage, Alain Graillot

Jura
Château Chalon, Jean Bourdy

Loire
Muscadet de Sévres et Maine sur Lie,
Marquis de Goulaine
Pouilly Fumé, Jean-Claude Guyot
Reuilly, Domaine Claude Lafond
Sancerre, Domaine des Petits
Perriers, André Vatan
Savennières, Roche-aux-Moines,
Domaine aux Moines
Sauvignon Blanc, Domaine de la
Garrelière (Touraine)
Vouvray, Daniel Jarry

Provence
Cassis, Clos St Magdeleine, Côtes de
Provence
Palette Blanc, Château Simone, Aix-
en-Provence

Savoie
Chignin-Bergeron, Louis Magnin
Roussette de Savoie, Louis Magnin

AUSTRALIA
Ashbrook Estate Margaret River,
Chardonnay Verdelo Blend,
Western Australia
Chardonnay Petaluma Adelaide
Hills, South Australia
Grosset Riesling, Clare Valley, South
Australia
Leeuwin Estate Chardonnay Art
Series
Penfolds Yattarna Chardonnay
(White Grange)

AUSTRIA
Grüner Veitliner, Nikolaihof

CHILE
Santa Isabel Estate, Casablanca

ENGLAND
Breaky Bottom Seyval Blend, East
Sussex
Camel Valley, Cornwall
Chapel Down, New Wave Wines,
Kent

GERMANY
Rhine Riesling Spätlese Johannisholf
Schloss Reinhartshausen, Rheingau
(Kabinett)

GREECE
Oenoforos, Pelopponese

ITALY
Friuli-Venezia Giulia
Pinot Bianco Vittorio Puiatti
Pinot Grigio Collio, Vittorio Puiatti
Verduzzo, Giovanni Dri

Marches
Verdicchio, Castelli di Jesi

Piedmont
Gavi di Gavi, La Scolca

Veneto
Soave Classico Capitel. Foscarino,
Anselmi

NEW ZEALAND
Sauvignon Blanc, Cloudy Bay,
Marlborough
Sauvignon Blanc, Wairau River,
Marlborough

PORTUGAL
Vinho Verde, Quinta do Ermizio,
Douro

SPAIN
Rías Baixas, Do Ferreior, Galicia

SWITZERLAND
Chasselas, Desalay Lavaux, Vaud

USA
Ridge Santa Cruz Chardonnay,
California
Sanford Sauvignon Blanc, Santa
Barbara

ROSÉ WINES

FRANCE
Basque
Irouleguy Rosé, Domaine Ilarria

Provence
Bandol Rosé, Château Pibarnon
Bellet, Domaine de la Source,
J. Dalmasso
Domaine Gavoty, Cuvée Clarendon

Caves de Remoulins, Gard (Syrah)
Coteaux d'Aix-en-Provence,
Domaine des Béates (Grenache)

Loire
Rosé d'Anjou, Domaine de Pied
Flond

MOROCCO
Gris Castel, Fez

SPAIN
Bilbainas Bodegas Rioja Alta

RED WINES

FRANCE
Alsace
Pinor Noir, Léon Beyer

Ardèche
Gamay d'Archèche, Cave
Cooperative de Saint Sauveur
de Cruzières
Syrah, Louis Latour

Basque
Irouleguy, Mignaberry, Christian
Duvernet

Beaujolais
Brouilly Domaine Combillaty,
Georges Duboeuf
Morgon, Domaine Piron

Bordeaux
St Julien
Château Gruaud Larose

Pauillac
Château d'Armailhac
Château Lafite Rothschild
Château Pichon Comtesse de Lalande
Grand Vin de Château Latour

Margaux
Château Labégorce-Zédé
Château Margaux

Graves
Château Haut Brion
Château La Mission Haut-Brion

St Emillon
Château l'Angélus
Chateau Ausone
Château Le Castelot
Château Cheval Blanc
Château Vieux Sarpe

Pomerol
Château La Croix St Georges
Le Pin
Pétrus
Vieux Château Certan

Burgundy
Beaune Greves, Vignes de l'Enfant
  Jesus, Bouchard Père et Fils
Clos Saint Denis, Domaine Dujac
Corton, Le Rognet, Domaine
  Chevalier
La Tâche, Domaine de la Romanée
  Conti
Latricières Chambertin, Domaine
  Faiveley
Musigny Vielles Vignes, Domaine
  de Vogüé
Nuits St Georges, Les Pruliers,
  Domaine R. Chevillon
Rully, Domaine Faively
Romanée Conti, Domaine de la
  Romanée Conti
Richebourg, Domaine de la
  Romanée Conti
Vosne Romanée 1er Cru Cros
  Parantoux, Henri Jayer

Cahors
Le Cedre, Château du Cédre
Cahors Clos Triguedina, Prince
  Probus

Corbières
Château Auris, Cuvée Prestige

Côtes de Provence
Domaine Tempier, Cuvée Special
  La Migoua (Bandol)

Côtes du Rhône
Châteauneuf du Pâpe, Clos de Pâpes
  Paul Avril
Côte Rôtie, Robert Jasmin
Côtes du Rhône Villages, Esprit de
  Terroirs, Vigneron de Chusclan
Crozes Hermitage, Chapoutier

Crozes Hermitage, M. Alain Graillot
Saint Joseph, Jean Louis Grippat

Loire
Cabernet de Touraine, Domaine
  Thierry Michaud (Bourgeuil)
Chinon, Château de Coulaine
Sancerre, Pascal Jolivet
Saumur Champigny Vieilles Vignes,
  Domaine Filliatreau

Savoie
Mondeuse, Prestige, Domaine
  Prieuré St Christophe .R et M
  Grisard
Gamay de Savoie, Famille Edmont
  Jachquin et Fils

ARGENTINA
Malbec, Bodega Noemia
Tempranillo, O Fournier Valle de
  Uco Bodega

AUSTRALIA
Brokenwood Hunter Valley Shiraz
Penfolds RWT Shiraz, South
  Australia
Penfolds Magill Estate Shiraz
Penfolds Grange, Bin 95

CHILE
Cabernet Sauvignon, Don Melchor,
  Chile

ITALY
Piedmont
Barbaresco, Gaja
Barolo Cannubi Boschis, L. Sandrone
Dolcetto d'Alba, Aldo Conterno

Tuscany
Chianti Classico Riserva, Castello di
  Brolio
Sassicaia, Tenuta San Guido, Incisa
  della Rochetta
Tignanello Antinori

Veneto
Amarone Della Valpolicell, Masi
Valpolicella, Classico Allegrini

NEW ZEALAND
Pinot Noir, Felton Road Block 5,
  Otago

SOUTH AFRICA
Kanonkop Pinotage
Fairview, Primo Pinotage

SPAIN
Ribera del Duero
Pingus
Vega Sicilia "Unico"

Rioja
Solar de Amezola Rioja Gran Reserva

Penedes
Torres Gran Coronas, Mas La Plana

SWITZERLAND
Pinot Dole Blanche Martigny
Pinot Noir, Oeil de Perdrix, Neuchâtel

USA
Merlot, Firestone, Santa Barbara
Opus One, Robert Mondavi, Napa
Pinot Noir, Domaine Drouhin, Oregon
Zinfandel, Robert Mondavi, Napa

SWEET AND FORTIFIED WINES

FRANCE
Barsac, Château Climens
Barsac, Château Coutet
Banyuls, Reserva, Domaine la Tour
  Vielle
Banyuls, Vin de Meditation, Domaine
  la Tour Vielle
Bonnezeau La Chapelle, Gaston
  Lenotre (Coteaux-du-Layon)
Gewürztraminer, Sélection de Grains
  Nobles, Hugel
Gewürztraminer, Sélection de Grains
  Nobles, Léon Beyer
Maury, Mas Amiel, Réserve
Muscat de Beaumes de Venise,
  Domaine Durban
Muscat de Frontignan, La Peyrade
Muscat de Lunel, Domaine Clos
  Bellevue
Muscat de Rivesaltes, Cazes Frères
Muscat Cap Corse, Antoine Arena
Jurançon, Symphonie de Novembre,
  Domaine Cauhapé
Pacherenc du Vic, Bilh, Brumaire,
  A. Brumon

Pineau de Charentes, Château de
  Beaulon (5 years old)
Rasteau, Caves des Vignerons,
  Domaine Didier Charvin
Sauternes, Château Filhot
Sauternes, Château Gilette,
  Crème de Tête
Sauternes, Château d'Yquem
  Lur-Saluces
Sauternes, Château Suduiraut
Sauternes, Château Lafaurie
  Peyraguey
Sauternes, Clos Dady
Tokay Pinot Gris, Sélection de Grains
  Nobles, Léon Beyer
Vin de Paille, Gerard Chave,
  Domaine Monin
Vouvray, Le Haut Lieu, Moelleux,
  G. Huet

AUSTRALIA
De Bortoli Griffith Botrytis
  Semillon, NSW
Hill Smith Estate Botrytis Riesling,
  NSW
Primo Estate Botrytis Riesling,
  Adelaide
Rutherglen Muscat, Victoria

AUSTRIA
Trockenbeerenauslese, Hoppler

CANADA
Icewine, Inniskillin

GERMANY
Grans Fassian Eiswein, Mosel
Golberg Rulander Beerenauslese,
  Max Reinhold

GREECE
Samos Muscat de Samos, Co-op de
  Samos

HUNGARY
The Royal Tokaji Wine Company

ITALY
Recioto di Soave Roberto Anselmi,
  Veneto
Recioto della Valpolicella Allegrini,
  Veneto
Visciolata (cherry-flavoured wine),
  Bologna

SOUTH AFRICA
De Wetshof Estate, Danie de Wet
  Cape Muscadel
Boplaas Port, Calitzdorp
Vin de Constance, Klein Constantia
  Estate

SPAIN AND PORTUGAL
Cossart Gordon Bual Madeira
Blandy's Special Solera 1860 Madeira
Bodegas Schenk, Valencia (Moscatel)
Churchill White Port
Quinta do Noval Port
Sandeman Ruby Port
Sandeman LBV Port
Warre's Port
Amontillado Lustau's Almacenista
  Sherry
Fino Gonzalez Byass Sherry
Manzanilla Hidalgos La Gitana
  Sherry
Matusalem Gonzalez Byass Sherry
Oloroso Rio Viejo Domecq Sherry

UKRAINE
Massandra Collection 'Red Port'
  Crimea

BEER AND CIDER

Belgian Fruit Beer
Kriek Lambic Cantillon
Lindeman's Framboise, Flanders

Brown Ale
Wadworth Old Timer

India Pale Ale
Bass Ale
Cobbold IPA
Park Slope, USA
Young's London Ale

Lager
Hoepfner Pilsner Baden-
  Württemberg

Light Dry Larger
Le Gavroche, Pas-de-Calais, France
Tsingtao, China

Old Ale
Hobgoblin
Theakston Old Peculiar

Rodenbach Beer
Rodenbach Grand Cru

Stout
Gorden Highland Scotch ale

White Lager
La Choulette, Northern France

Cider
Westons Organic Cider (bottle
  conditioned)
Dunkerton Organic (sweet cider)

SPIRITS

Amaretto
Disarono

Grappa
Jacopo Poli

Rum
Santa Teresa Ron Antiguo de Solera,
  Venezuela

Whisky
Macallan Single Highland Malt,
  10 years old
Dewar Rattray individual cask
  bottled
Aberlour Single Malt Speyside

Blended Whisky
Johnny Walker Black Label

Vodka
Grey Goose

Index

A la santé du chef

Acknowledgements

My thanks to my parents for wedging my nose into
a glass of Yquem as a child; to everyone at Weidenfeld
& Nicolson, namely Susan Haynes, Jinny Johnson,
David Rowley and Clive Hayball; Marion my secretary,
who once again had to put up with my doctor's writing;
Monica Galetti for helping with the food photography
and not forgetting Tara, the once again very heavily
pregnant photographer; Silvano Giraldin whose
knowledge and expertise was a major contribution along
with François Bertrand. I'd also like to thank all the
vineyards who have supplied labels of their wines for
us to feature in the book.

And a special thanks to Mr Zdenek J. Gregor who saved
my sight in my left eye.

Half-title page:
A family photograph. Michel at table, aged 5.

First published in the United Kingdom in 2005 by
Weidenfeld & Nicolson
an imprint of the Orion Publishing Group
Wellington House
125 Strand
London WC2R 0BB

Text copyright © Michel Roux Jr 2005
Design and layout © Weidenfeld & Nicolson 2005

Photographs by Tara Fisher

A CIP catalogue record for this book is available from
the British Library

ISBN 0 297 84327 3

Printed and bound in Italy

Design director David Rowley
Editorial director Susan Haynes
Designed by Clive Hayball
Edited by Jinny Johnson
Proofread by Connie Novis
Index by Elizabeth Wiggans